First
Aid

External Features of the Cat

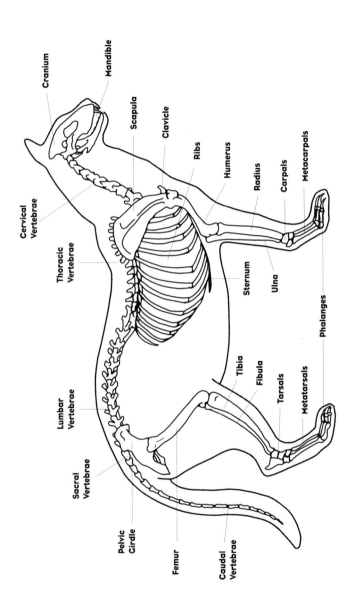

Cranium

Mandible

Cervical
Vertebrae

Scapula

Clavicle

Ribs

Humerus

Radius

Carpals

Metacarpals

Thoracic
Vertebrae

Sternum

Ulna

Phalanges

Lumbar
Vertebrae

Tibia

Fibula

Tarsals

Metatarsals

Sacral
Vertebrae

Pelvic
Girdle

Femur

Caudal
Vertebrae

What Is First Aid?

"First aid" is the first response to aid a cat in an emergency situation. Depending on the specific injury or illness, the cat may need only simple intervention to become stabilized. At the other extreme, there may be little anyone can do at the scene and immediate transfer to the nearest veterinary facility may be the best first aid.

There are many types of emergencies and some are more immediately life threatening than others. Compare, for example, the severity between a cat that has broken his tail with a cat that has been hit by a car. A tail is not a vital organ and although the injury may be quite painful, it is unlikely to be life-threatening. A cat that has been hit by a car can suffer injuries that may range from minimal (perhaps only a few scrapes) to severe (such as internal bleeding) if the cat is lucky enough to survive the impact at all.

The Goals of First Aid

The primary goal of first aid is to take immediate and appropriate action to preserve the life of the patient.

First aid is most valuable in extreme emergency situations when failure to respond could result in the cat's death.

The second goal of first aid is to prevent further deterioration of the cat. As soon as a physical problem becomes apparent, appropriate intervention is required to keep

Assess your cat's health every day to establish a baseline for comparison in the event that an emergency situation occurs.

things from getting worse until trained professionals have the opportunity to intervene.

The third goal of first aid is to relieve pain and discomfort. Pain is not necessarily a reliable indication of the severity of an injury or illness. Causing some pain to an injured cat may be unavoidable during first aid, for example, when the cat is gently lifted into your car for transport to the clinic. Moreover, it might not be advisable to relieve pain completely in an injured animal because the cat will likely try to move around before healing is complete.

And finally, the fourth goal of first aid is to ensure the health of the cat with immediate veterinary attention. The purpose of this book is not to teach everything there is to know about veterinary emergency medicine and care. As a devoted and concerned cat owner, it is important that you understand the basics of the most commonly encountered veterinary emergencies. In many situations, you will be able to make a difference by responding appropriately to help your sick or injured pet. But unless you are a veterinarian, you should not make decisions regarding your pet's safety or survival without the benefit of first-hand veterinary attention. First aid should be directed at your cat's initial care in the actual emergency situation or as soon as a problem is discovered. In almost every case, first aid should not replace subsequent veterinary attention.

First Aid Kit

The following items are easily obtained from your local pharmacy. You should store them in a moisture proof container that is easily accessible in an emergency (but out of reach of children and pets). In addition, include a list of emergency telephone numbers on an index card. You may want to have this laminated or place it inside a plastic cover. You might also include a copy of this book for quick reference as necessary. Think about making a duplicate kit to keep with you in the car in case something happens when you are away from home. If you often travel with your cat, research the availability of emergency veterinary coverage at your destination. The better prepared you are, the less likely you are to panic in case of an emergency.

THE CONTENTS OF YOUR FIRST AID KIT

- Two rolls of gauze: One roll that is 2 inches and one roll that is 3 or 4 inches in width
- White "surgical" tape, 1 inch in width
- Two rolls of elastic wrap, one roll that is 2 inches in width and one roll that is 3 or 4 inches in width
- One roll of cotton batting (12 inches in width)
- An emergency ice pack
- A bottle of 1 percent hydrogen peroxide
- Box of exam gloves
- A pillow case (to transport)
- A blanket (for warmth)
- A towel (for a splint)
- A bottle of saline eye wash
- Two rectal thermometers
- A pair of blunt-tipped scissors
- A pair of tweezers
- A flashlight
- A bottle of antihistamine
- A box of baking soda

Practice Before an Emergency

Practicing before an emergency can be a vital investment:

- The more comfortable you are in using the contents of the first aid kit, the more smoothly you can respond should the need arise.

- If your pet is cooperative, you could try making leg bandages or taking his temperature. (It is likely that your cat will be impatient with your unfamiliar manipulations, however; you could practice bandaging on a stuffed animal.)

- Practice lifting and carrying your cat according to the suggestions you will read later on in this book.

- Practice driving the route to your nearest veterinary emergency facility.

- Establish a professional relationship with the clinic and keep emergency telephone numbers handy (for example, in your wallet, in your car and on your refrigerator).

- Review this book periodically to keep basic concepts fresh in your mind.

How to Approach a Frightened or Injured Cat

In a medical emergency, an injured cat that remains conscious will almost certainly be in a state of extreme fear. Any pain or disability that he may be experiencing will further amplify his anxiety. The animal's natural response will be to try to escape the scene of an accident and to seek shelter in a location where he will feel less vulnerable. Pain and confusion may lead to panic. If he is able to do so, an injured or frightened pet may try to run away if someone approaches, even if that individual is trying to help and even if it is you.

The powerful natural instinct to flee or to stand and fight can be even more pronounced in an injured or sick pet. Outdoors, an injured and panicking cat can easily get lost or worsen his injuries in an attempt to escape from what he perceives to be a menacing person. House cats may hide in very difficult to reach places in the home or in other effective hideouts. If the animal feels unable to escape the advance of a potentially harmful person, he may become aggressive, and thus injured or ill animals can be extremely dangerous. These pets must be approached slowly and with great care so as not to aggravate their state of anxiety or to trigger an attack. To approach a cat in an emergency situation (regardless of whether he is obviously afraid), do the following:

**MAKE AND KEEP
REGULAR VETERINARY
APPOINTMENTS**

An effective way to prevent a health crisis is to make regular veterinary appointments for your cat. Your veterinarian may discover changes in your cat's health status that you have overlooked. He or she will also keep your cat's vaccinations up-to-date—a critical factor in keeping your cat well.

• Move toward the animal in a steady and very slow pace. Even if the injured or sick cat is your own, avoid the urge to rush to his aid because you could make the situation a lot worse for everyone.

• Keep your arms at your side and avoid sudden movements that could amplify a vulnerable cat's feeling of panic.

To approach an injured and aggressive cat, crouch down and slowly advance behind a large towel or blanket; wrap the cat completely and tuck him under your arm.

• Avoid direct eye contact with the cat. An animal that is in poor physical condition and unable to defend himself may perceive this as a threat. Instead, avert your gaze to a point slightly past the animal's shoulder.

• Keep your voice soft and soothing. With your calming tone and reassuring words, you may avoid

alarming the animal further and he might wel-
come your approach. Remember that our pets
learn to become expert judges of our moods by
our body language and verbal intonations. If you
project an image of anxiety and panic, the vulnerable animal will become even more defensive.

- If the animal seems to panic increasingly as you
come closer, crouch down and stay where you are
for a moment. Continue trying to reassure him
with your voice before beginning your approach
again. If the cat remains agitated or alarmed in any
way, it may be necessary to crawl toward him and
avoid looking in his direction altogether. Stop your
advance every few feet to allow the animal to adjust
to your presence. Proceed with caution.

*A breakaway or
an elastic collar
with identifica-
tion tags is
important for
outdoor cats and
even for those
that stay inside,
just in case.*

- If the cat is obviously fearful and aggressive (e.g.,
hissing, growling, hair standing on end, tail swish-
ing violently, ears flattened against the head),
resist your urge to reach toward him with your
hand. Instead, stay where you are for a few
moments longer and remain motionless as you
continue talking in a soothing manner. If the cat
remains agitated, back away to a distance at which
he seems to relax or at least reduces his aggressive
displays. Never jeopardize your own safety.

- Another way to approach a cat that does not relax his guard is to use a blanket, sheet or towel as a blind. Open the blanket with your arms held wide so that it covers you but does not quite obstruct your view. When you are close enough, drop the blanket over the injured animal and especially over his head and front paws. Cats will instinctively lash out with their front paws but will also kick with their rear paws, claws unsheathed. You must be aware of the claws on their feet as well as their teeth. Cats that have been declawed of their front claws are no more likely to bite than are other cats but can still harm you or startle you enough to make their getaway. Firmly collect the cat in your arms with the blanket rolled around and beneath his body (to minimize contact of their "weapons" with your skin). Sometimes, the only thing to do may be to completely envelop the injured and aggressive cat in the blanket or towel and transport your patient in this makeshift "bag."

> ### KEEP YOUR SICK (AND HEALTHY) CAT INDOORS
>
> If your cat normally roams outdoors, it is important to keep him inside as soon as you discover any injury or sudden illness. Keeping your cat inside when he is ill will allow you to monitor his condition and have him treated by your veterinarian. Should you continue to let him go outdoors, he may run away and become more ill due to environmental exposure and lack of veterinary care. Sick cats can become disoriented and lost before you are aware that their health is compromised. They are far more susceptible to additional hazards such as animal attacks or traffic because their reaction time is slower than normal. You may want to consider keeping your cat indoors indefinitely. House cats are protected from a long list of potential health problems and diseases, including rabies, that are contagious to people. Pamper your cat when he is ill and when he is healthy, too!

- Another way to contain the cat is with a pillow case (easy to store in your first aid kit); you might also wish to keep a nylon gym bag to use for emergency transport. Secure the pillowcase with an elastic band or tie off with a knot (your cat will breathe nicely through this material). Capture your patient as safely (for you both) as possible and place him in the pillowcase or gym bag for immediate transfer to the veterinary clinic.

- If you feel unable to safely approach the victim or even if you simply lack the confidence to offer assistance, get help. Go to the nearest telephone and call a friend, an animal shelter, animal control officer or veterinary clinic for their advice and possible intervention at the scene.

chapter 2

Basics of First Aid

If you think that it might be an emergency, then it is. No one knows better than you do what constitutes an emergency situation. You know your cat's normal habits and behavior, including her moods, facial expressions, bowel and bladder habits and appetite. You should call your veterinary clinic and describe your pet's symptoms with any of your concerns for her well-being. It is always better to err on the side of caution. The hospital staff is trained to recognize when an animal should be seen on an immediate emergency basis, or as

a fit-in appointment within twenty-four hours or as a regular appointment within several days. If the staff seems to think there is no immediate danger to your pet despite your concern, leave a message to speak with your veterinarian.

13

In general, you should *seek immediate veterinary care* if your cat:

- has been hit by a car (even without obvious injury)

- has suffered any type of traumatic injury (e.g. cat fight, fall from heights, sudden lameness) or, even in the absence of obvious injury, has survived any type of traumatic event (such as being a passenger in a car that was in an automobile accident)

- has lost consciousness even briefly, regardless of the cause

- is bleeding uncontrollably (even after ice and/or pressure is applied)

- has difficulty walking

- has difficulty breathing

- has difficulty urinating (strains or cries when urinating, unable to void urine or bloody urine)

- has diarrhea with blood.

As a rule, you should make an *appointment to be seen within twenty-four hours* if your cat:

- seems to be in minor discomfort (e.g. chews at her feet, scratches more than usual, limps a bit) and/or is behaving unusually (e.g. is socially withdrawn, has lost her appetite)

- has an already recognized medical condition of any kind and is showing physical changes or is behaving unusually

- is currently on any medication and is showing physical changes or is behaving unusually

- has a minor traumatic injury that initially responds to your first aid

- has difficulty seeing (squinting, tearing, discharge, itchiness) from one or both eyes

- has difficulty defecating (strains or vocalizes when attempting to defecate, absence of stools for more than twenty-four hours, small amount of blood on formed stools) or has diarrhea.

If you have any doubts as to the severity of a problem, have your pet seen on an emergency basis. *Trust your instincts.* Acting quickly may prevent a minor emergency from escalating into a major problem. Perhaps the single most important thing to do to prevent an emergency is to *call your veterinary clinic as soon as you detect a problem with your cat.*

Monitoring Breathing

There are a number of ways to monitor a cat's breathing (respiration). Practice evaluating your cat's normal breathing before an emergency situation arises. It is important to recognize several characteristics that qualify breathing.

FREQUENCY (RESPIRATORY RATE)

Small cats breathe faster than larger ones and the rate of any cat's breathing will increase after exercise and in times of stress. The normal respiratory rate is roughly between twenty to thirty breaths per minute. To evaluate your cat's rate of breathing, watch the rise and fall of your cat's chest. When she inhales, the chest will rise as the lungs fill with air and use the essential oxygen it carries. When she exhales, the chest will fall as air moves out and takes with it carbon dioxide gas that is produced as a by-product of metabolism. When you count the respiratory frequency, count either the number of times your cat inhales (chest rises) or exhales (chest falls) over a sixty-second period. A shortcut is to count the frequency over a thirty-second interval and multiply by two (respirations/minute).

> **NEVER HESITATE TO CONTACT YOUR VETERINARIAN**
>
> Please do not feel that your perception of a potential problem involving your cat is only imaginary or unimportant. One of the greatest frustrations of veterinary practice is being confronted with a problem that the pet has endured for an unnecessarily long time. Some conditions become increasingly difficult to treat even after just a few days are allowed to pass. It is never inappropriate to call and speak to your veterinarian. His or her primary concern, like yours, is the well-being of your pet.

It can be difficult to assess breathing only by sight. In an emergency, respirations may be shallow or even absent (see the discussion of artificial respiration later in this chapter) and can be hard to evaluate in a very heavy cat or a cat with a thick, long coat. Rather than observing the chest movement, place your hand or face within 1 or 2 inches of the cat's nostrils to feel the warm breath as it is exhaled through the nose. Try this with a small mirror and you will see water vapor condense on the mirror's surface as the animal exhales. Another simple technique is to place your hand lightly on the cat's chest over the ribs midway between her forearm and abdomen to feel the cat's breathing motions.

An easy way to monitor breathing is to place your hand lightly on the cat's chest.

QUALITY

Watch and listen to your cat when she is resting comfortably. In general, normal respiration through the nostrils is almost silent (unless the cat has a short muzzle and restricted nostrils such as a Persian). In open-mouthed breathing (panting), seen in cats that are very hot, stressed or that have cardiopulmonary disease, the breathing sounds are more audible. A wheezing sound, however, might indicate a restricted airway. A gurgling sound with each respiration is suggestive of some type of fluid in the respiratory system. In a sick or injured cat, for example, it would be important to report to your veterinarian that the breathing sounded harsh, or heavier than usual, or that there was a yellow or perhaps a bloody discharge from the cat's nostrils.

EFFORT

In the well cat, breathing should be an involuntary function. In other words, breathing should be effortless and accomplished unconsciously by the individual cat. In some emergencies and diseases, breathing is so affected that it is no longer an automatic or painless function. In these cases, breathing is described as "labored" if the pet seems to struggle for breath. Rather than the normal, gentle rise and fall of the chest and ribs with each breath, these movements may appear forced and erratic. The greater the difficulty encountered with each breath, the more likely the cat will pant with her mouth open. The cat's facial expression may reflect her anxiety. In extreme cases, the abdomen appears to pump up and down as the chest heaves with each breath. This is called costoabdominal respiration and is not normal breathing.

Cats with short muzzles, such as Persians, may naturally make noise when they breathe.

Monitoring Heartbeat

The normal feline heart rate (cardiac frequency) ranges between 110 to 140 beats per minute. Heart rate in cats depends on a variety of factors, such as the size of the cat, her age, physical fitness and emotional state. For example, the heart may beat as fast as 200 beats per minute in young kittens. A healthy adult cat of average size may have a resting heart rate of about 120 beats per minute, but the rate will accelerate if the cat sees an unfamiliar dog, hears the hum of your electric can opener or chases a mouse.

The heart rate will also increase when the body temperature rises due to fever, for example, or when the cat's blood pressure falls due to shock. In a state of medical emergency, a cat may panic or become restless due to pain and the heart rate may rise. Some diseases, such as hyperthyroidism, will also increase the resting heart rate in cats. Heart rate will decrease in a state of rest but it can also fall because the animal is ill. Internal hemorrhage, for example, may initially trigger an increase in heart rate as the body tries to stabilize itself, but if it can no longer compensate for an important loss of blood volume, the heart rate may drop.

To monitor heart rate, practice on your cat when she is at rest even before an emergency occurs. With the cat lying on her right side, bend the left elbow slightly by pressing back against her paw. The elbow will lie just in front of the heart in this position. Rest your hand lightly on the chest wall just behind the left elbow to feel the heart beat. This is the position where the heart

muscle comes closest to the body's surface. The heart can be felt on the right side in the same location but not as strongly as on the left side, unless the cat is very small, narrow-chested or very young. Ideally, the heart rate should be monitored for a full sixty seconds, but in an emergency this is not always possible. To measure cardiac frequency, count the frequency over a twenty-second interval and multiply by three to obtain the heart rate per minute. Counting over thirty seconds then multiplying by two, however, may give you a more accurate count.

To monitor your cat's heart rate, bend her left elbow and place your hand on the chest just behind the point of the elbow.

Signs of Shock

Shock is a physiological phenomenon that results in cardiovascular collapse. Unfortunately, although its function is to defend vital organ systems in an emergency, a cat can die of the consequences of shock before she succumbs to the effects of her injuries. Gum color and capillary refill, mental status (alert, sluggish, comatose), heart rate and body temperature are all important reflections of the state of shock.

To evaluate signs of shock, the cat's cardiovascular system must be assessed. This is done by physical examination that you can do at the scene of an emergency. One of the basic signs of shock is a slower capillary refill time. To evaluate your cat's rate of capillary refill:

1. Lift the side of the cat's mouth to expose the gums.

2. Gently but firmly press one finger into the gums for one to two seconds (you will notice that the pressure of your finger blocks blood circulation beneath your finger tip so that the gums appear pale) and remove your finger.

3. Observe how long it takes for the blanched zone to regain a normal pink color or to return to the same appearance of the gums around it (anything slower than two seconds is a sign of a problem).

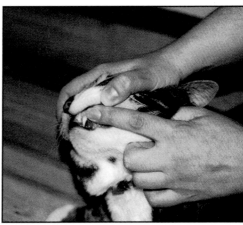

Warning: Your pet may be in early shock and have normal gum color. Do not dismiss the severity of your cat's condition even if she does not seem in shock to you at the time—bring her to the veterinary clinic to be certain that no treatment is necessary. It is most important to note your pet's mental status. If your cat seems sluggish, slow to respond to you or lethargic and confused, she should be transported to a clinic immediately. If your cat has lost consciousness, do not waste time by examining her for more minor signs of shock.

To evaluate your cat for shock, start by lifting her mouth to expose the gums; then press on the gums firmly and observe how long it takes for the blanched area to regain a pink color.

Shock can be caused by many different injuries and diseases, but there are common findings. In general, the shock patient will be weak, subdued or even comatose. Her pulse may be rapid and weak. Her body temperature may be below normal but may also be normal or even above normal (for example, in the case of shock secondary to bacterial infection). There are three important categories of medical emergencies resulting in shock:

1. **Hypovolemic shock**—anything that causes a reduction of normal blood volume (such as hemorrhage, trauma or dehydration) can lead to this

type of shock; gums and other membranes (e.g. inside lining of the eyelids) will be pale and cool.

2. **Low blood pressure**—secondary to central nervous system (brain) disorders or trauma, as well as extreme allergic reactions (anaphylaxis) and drug reactions can result in shock with unusually pink and warm gums.

3. **Shock due to infection** (Septicemia)—can result from bacterial, viral or fungal infections but can also develop from the other types of shock above; gums may be blanched but may also appear muddy.

Animals in shock may breathe rapidly but not take deep breaths (hyperventilation). They may be panicked and agitated following an accident. In early stages, the body's defense mechanisms will try to rally to allow an injured or sick cat to escape danger. As these defenses progress, however, signs of shock will become more obvious and extreme, leading to collapse. If your cat is conscious, keep her calm and reassured with your tone of voice. If she is unconscious or seems disoriented following any kind of accident proceed to your veterinary clinic *immediately*. Cover her with a towel or blanket or any article of clothing you can spare to maintain her body temperature. If injuries appear superficial or minor (a scratch, for example) yet your cat seems dazed and unable to rise, ignore the scratches and transport her to the clinic *immediately*. If the injury bleeds profusely or if the animal is increasingly lethargic or unconscious, apply first aid to control bleeding and see your veterinarian *immediately*.

Taking Body Temperature

A cat's normal body temperature is generally between 100 and 103°F (37.5–39.5°C). The best way to take a measurement of a cat's body temperature is with a rectal thermometer. You may purchase a rectal thermometer at any pharmacy. These are available in the traditional glass version or in digital models. If you drop a glass thermometer, it will shatter and the liquid mercury it contains will spill tiny droplets that can be challenging to retrieve. It also takes about one minute to get an accurate reading. The glass thermometer is inexpensive and accurate, but should be used with care. Digital models are a bit more costly but give faster readings (within thirty seconds or less) and are fairly accurate. The major disadvantage of relying on a digital thermometer is that the battery may have worn out just when you need to take your pet's temperature. It may be safest to keep one of each type of thermometer (or two of the same type) in your emergency kit and bathroom cabinet, just in case. To measure your cat's temperature:

1. Shake the glass thermometer down so that it reads less than 99°F; (this is unnecessary with a digital version). *Note:* In a real emergency, it would be important to shake it down even lower than 99°F, because body temperature can fall to dangerously low levels.

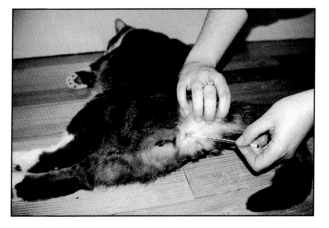

To measure your cat's body temperature, gently lift the tail, place the lubricated tip of the thermometer against the anus, carefully insert and gently hold in place for one minute.

2. Lubricate the thermometer tip with a drop of lubricating jelly, petroleum jelly, liquid soap or detergent.

3. Gently raise the cat's tail (Manx cats have no tail or your cat may have had her tail amputated) so that the anus is exposed. If necessary, part the hair so that you have a clear view of your target.

4. Place the thermometer tip against the anus. You may notice that the anal sphincter may tense momentarily, as if it is winking at you.

5. When the "winking" slows a bit, gradually insert the thermometer approximately 1 inch into the rectum (approximately ¼ to ½ of the length of the instrument). Depending on the type of thermometer you use, leave the instrument in for about thirty to sixty seconds. With a glass thermometer, you can watch as the mercury rises for about one minute, but when it seems to have stopped, your reading is usually complete. With a digital instrument, you will hear a beep when the measurement is done.

6. Slowly withdraw the thermometer and wipe with a tissue or cotton ball. If you are not in an emergency situation, disinfect the thermometer with some soap and water or wipe it again with alcohol before you store it away. In an emergency, you can worry about this detail later!

If you practice with a healthy and alert cat, taking a temperature may be resented so do not insist. This should not be a painful procedure if it is done correctly and with consideration, and it provides vital information regarding your cat's condition. However, *in a life-threatening emergency, taking a body temperature can be skipped in the interest of speeding your cat to an emergency facility.*

Disinfecting Wounds

Wounds at the body surface can be open or closed. Open wounds include cuts (lacerations), scrapes (abrasions), punctures, draining abscesses and open fractures (bone fragments that penetrate the skin to the outside). Closed wounds include bruises (hematoma), closed abscesses, closed fractures and soft tissue injuries such as sprains (joint torsion). Do not attempt to remove an embedded foreign body (debris of any size, knife, wood, metal object) because massive hemorrhage may follow. Instead, keep your cat calm and

warm and proceed immediately to the nearest veterinary facility.

Before you disinfect your cat's injuries, examine her
more closely. Are there any bones or muscle exposed?
If so, the injury is serious and you should proceed to
the nearest veterinary facility for treatment. Is your pet
becoming agitated or even aggressive when you
attempt to examine the wound? Do not risk injury to
yourself by trying to disinfect the wound. Leave this to
trained professionals.

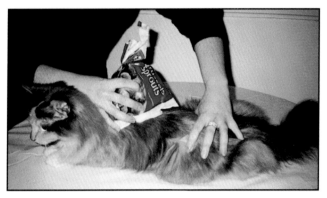

*An ice pack can
be made from ice
cubes or even
from a bag of
frozen vegetables.*

In many cases, an animal may be injured but the skin
is not broken. All you may see is some swelling, pain
and perhaps discoloration (deep pink to dark purple)
at the injured area. It is generally unnecessary to disinfect this type of injury and the most appropriate
thing to do is to apply an ice pack to the swollen area.
Whether a wound is open or closed, direct application
of ice is almost always helpful and the sooner it is
applied, the better. Ice is helpful to minimize swelling
(edema), pain and bleeding (hemorrhage). Use an ice
pack wrapped in a light cloth or cover the pack with
plastic and place it on the wound. Gel-filled flexible ice
packs can be purchased at any pharmacy, stored in the
freezer and kept ready for use, while chemical ice
packs need not be refrigerated and are activated by
manipulation. If no ice pack is available, a plastic bag
filled with ice cubes is an easy alternative to cover or
wrap around the injury. Another option is to use a bag
of frozen vegetables (frozen corn or peas work best but

any kind will do), which conforms nicely to almost any superficial injury.

If an open wound is bleeding, place a sterile gauze or clean cloth over the area and apply direct pressure to the surface. If you have an ice pack, use the ice pack applied with pressure directly to the wound. The combination of pressure and ice causes vessels to constrict and thereby minimize blood loss. If you do not have an ice pack, direct pressure alone will still be of great benefit.

Bleeding can originate from veins or from arteries of varying sizes. Large amounts of blood can be lost more quickly in arterial hemorrhage (especially if large vessels are damaged) than in hemorrhage from most veins.

If the bleeding seems to ooze onto the wound, the bleeding is probably from veins. Do not remove your pressure too soon or any clot that has formed may be torn away and hemorrhage could return. Arterial bleeding seems to pump in rhythm and this type of bleeding may be more difficult to control. Apply direct pressure and do not remove the pressure for at least five minutes.

If bleeding continues, seek veterinary care immediately. In fact, seek veterinary care right away for any open wound whether there is obvious bleeding or not.

If the bleeding wound is small (less than 2 inches or so), apply pressure directly with your fingers (direct manual pressure) over sterile gauze from your emergency kit. You may also use any clean towel or garment. If the wound is larger (greater than 2 inches), you may need to use your whole hand to stop the bleeding.

In general, soap and water remain the best way to clean most minor injuries such as cuts and scrapes. Use a basin of lukewarm water (tap water is acceptable in an emergency, sterile water is best if you have some), a soft face cloth, sponge or paper towel, with a small amount of liquid soap. As a second choice, or as a second step to disinfection, use hydrogen peroxide or betadine (proviodine 1 percent).

Do not rub the wound surface. Gently pour the cleansing solution over the wound directly from the basin or container, or soak a sponge or cloth and squeeze the solution over the area. This will flush away most debris such as bits of gravel, dirt, grass or hair that might be adhering to the wound. If any debris remains, even after generous flushing, use tweezers or even a clean cotton swab to remove as much as you can.

Rinse well with generous amounts of lukewarm water to remove any soapsuds or debris that remain on or in the wound. You may apply topical antibiotic (available through your veterinarian or your local pharmacy) to the wound surface. Apply a light dressing until a veterinarian can evaluate the injury.

Avoid touching the wound with your bare hands. By keeping your hands away from the wound, you will decrease the risk of infection to your pet and also protect yourself. Many diseases (such as rabies), are transmitted by direct contact with saliva or blood, and you must consider your own safety, particularly when the origin of the wound is unknown or if it was caused by a wild animal or unfamiliar pet of any kind.

> ## VACCINATE YOUR CAT AGAINST RABIES
>
> If your pet has been in a fight with another animal or even if you are simply unsure how an open wound was caused, consult with your veterinarian immediately. Rabies is reported everywhere in the United States and elsewhere in the world, and occasionally epidemics will erupt. Keep your cat's rabies vaccine up-to-date regardless of whether a rabies epidemic is reported in your area (you would not want your cat to be the first reported case in a new outbreak). Even if your cat never goes outdoors, a rabies vaccine may be mandatory where you live.

It can also be helpful, although not mandatory in an emergency situation, to clip the hair around the wound prior to disinfection so that you can more easily monitor healing. With scissors sterilized in hot water or rubbing alcohol, carefully trim the hair (to about $\frac{1}{4}$ inch in length) using the very tips of a pair of blunt scissors about 1 to 2 inches all around the wound. It is not necessary to try to cut the hair very short, as doing so will increase the risk of cutting your cat. If your cat has a smooth short coat, it is probably not worthwhile to attempt to trim the hair. Your veterinarian uses clipper blades that are specifically intended for use on pets and do not harm the skin.

Applying Bandages and Splints

For first aid purposes, bandages and splints are intended to be temporary until expert veterinary care is available. Do not feel that your skills need to be perfect.

BANDAGES

Bandages are needed to:

- cover open wounds to prevent further contamination during transport to the veterinary clinic

- cover bleeding wounds while pressure is applied to control blood loss during transport to the veterinary clinic

- apply slight pressure to an injury to minimize swelling and the sensation of pain before (and after) treatment by a veterinarian

- prevent the cat from creating further harm by licking her own wounds before or after she has received veterinary care

- keep healing wounds clean and dry following veterinary care.

Flush away surface debris and disinfect before applying any bandage to an open wound. This may not always be possible in an emergency or even necessary (in the case of a hemorrhaging wound, for example). Apply a square gauze or a sterile non-stick pad large enough to cover the surface wound; if you only have small gauze pads, use several and overlap them to cover the wound; apply several layers to provide a thick dressing for protection and additional absorption. With one hand, hold the dressing to the wound and place the end of the roll of bandaging material across the dressing. Rolled gauze is preferred for use as the layer over the local dressing, but if you do not have rolled gauze you may use whatever bandage supplies you have.

Wrap the rolled bandage around the dressing, overlapping by about ⅔ of the width of the bandage material; extend the bandage 1 to 2 inches above and below the edges of the dressing. Do not pull on the bandaging material as you unravel it or the bandage will be too tight (you should be able to easily pass your finger under the edge of the bandage).

If your intent is to apply a pressure bandage to control swelling or bleeding, create a bandage of many layers (use cotton batting in a roll for best results) so that the thickness of the bandage, not the tension, provides the desired pressure.

Use adhesive tape (preferably bandage or surgical tape) to secure the end of the bandage; if you will also be applying additional layers of bandage material (e.g. elastic bandage), it is unnecessary to tape the gauze wrap. If you have an elastic bandage available, apply it loosely, overlapping edges ⅔ of the width of the bandage; cover the inside layers of gauze and extend it about 1 inch beyond the edges of the gauze layer. Secure the end with tape or safety pins (many bandages, available at your local pharmacy, now come with fasteners or are self-adhesive). Use surgical or adhesive tape to cover the top inch of the bandage and 1 inch above the top of the bandage (this is the key to keeping the bandage in place—the adhesive tape must stick to hair or skin so that it will not slip—repeat application of the adhesive tape on the bottom edge of the bandage.

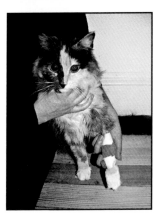

After disinfecting the wound, apply layers of gauze dressing, rolled gauze, bandaging and adhesive tape (do not pull tightly as you wrap or blood circulation may be impaired and cause pain and swelling).

Whenever possible, call ahead to warn the veterinary team that you are on the way with an injured cat; remain calm and proceed directly to the clinic.

27

SPLINTS

Splints are recommended if there is an obvious or suspected closed fracture, an open fracture or a large gaping wound on a limb. Do not touch any open wound with your bare hands.

An open fracture is one in which the bone fragments protrude at the skin surface. If there is an open fracture or wound, flush debris from the surface (see "Disinfecting Wounds," earlier in this chapter), place a clean dressing and, if possible, cover with a sterile dressing and light bandage before splinting the leg. If the wound is bleeding profusely, an ice pack can be bandaged tightly in place at the site of the hemorrhage and the limb immobilized with a splint.

A closed fracture should be suspected if your cat has pain and difficulty on attempts to walk using the injured leg. The fractured limb may be dragged, held off the ground, or simply held in awkward positions so that it does not bear the cat's weight. Some types of fractures are stable—the bone fragments are still held together (like pieces of a jigsaw, they interlock but are not solidly in place) and the cat gingerly may bear weight on the limb. In general, however, the pain of broken bones will deter voluntary movement of the limb. (It should be noted that some severe sprains and other soft tissue injuries can be painful enough initially to disable the limb.)

Although splints are helpful, they should be considered optional first aid. If the cat is able to bear weight on the leg or to control the injured limb (even if it is only to hold it flexed closer to the body) it is probably not worthwhile to make a splint. It would be helpful, with the severe injuries described above, to place a splint on a cat's leg if your cat allows you to do so! Moreover, a splint can help to minimize pain, bone displacement or other complications while you transport your cat for medical treatment. However, it is simply not worth wasting time if your pet panics, is very agitated or becomes aggressive while you try to fabricate a splint and maneuver her injured leg. Under these circumstances, proceed directly to the clinic. Call ahead, if possible, to let them know you will be arriving shortly with an emergency. Open fractures rank high in the list of urgent injuries and should be seen by your veterinarian *immediately.*

For the purposes of first aid, splints are intended as temporary bindings to stabilize an injury during transport. Splints are meant to immobilize an injured limb to minimize aggravation of the injury and pain and to provide support and cushioning. The splint can be made of improvised materials and secured with any type of adhesive tape, safety pins, a belt, string, ribbon, bandaging material or anything else you have available. Some common objects that can be used for splints include:

- A towel—fold the towel in half and, depending on the size of the towel and the size of the cat's leg, in half again; slide the folded towel under the leg and wrap it around toward the top of the leg (it need not encircle the leg entirely). Or, wrap the folded towel snugly but not tightly around the injured limb and secure it in place; it may be most comfortable simply to place the folded towel beneath the injured limb to provide support during transport.

- Any folded garment—the garment can be used as bandaging material to provide a bulky wrap or it can be folded and secured in the same way as the towel, above.

- Newspaper or magazine—a newspaper or magazine can be folded to provide a groove in which to rest the injured leg or it can be shaped into a roll and wrapped around the limb.

Make a temporary splint by folding a towel, wrapping it around the injured leg and securing it with a tie.

- Sticks/spoons—these can be tied directly to the length of the leg for short periods or can be used to provide additional support for bandages; Popsicle sticks may work perfectly for kittens.

- Boards/cardboard—almost any type of board (paper, wood, plastic, metal) can be used to support an injured limb as long as there are no sharp edges or splinters!

- Cardboard rolls from paper toweling (cardboard rolls from toilet paper for small cats and kittens)—the injured leg can be passed inside the roll and then a towel or cloth wrapped around the leg. The cardboard roll can be cut lengthwise to be more easily contoured to the leg and secured with tape.

How to Lift, Carry and Transport an Injured Cat

To lift a cat or kitten, hold the length of the cat's body close to you and grasp both of her front legs between your fingers; use your other hand to control her head and neck.

There are many methods of lifting an injured animal. You will need to consider the location of the emergency (e.g. in a ditch, in your yard, in a lake) in addition to the nature of your cat's injuries (unconscious, broken leg, bleeding wound). The size of the cat and her temperament are also important factors that will affect how she may be carried. Before you attempt to

lift any cat, be sure that you understand the suggestions for how to approach a frightened/injured cat set forth in chapter 1. Always remember to protect yourself from injury. You cannot help your cat if you are hurt in an attempt to rescue your cherished companion.

If your cat is able to walk but has an injured limb or other obvious injury, you may need to lift and carry her to your vehicle. Regardless of whether your cat is able to walk, avoid bending her body or making abrupt movements. Some injuries are undetectable at the accident scene.

The method of lifting your cat will depend greatly on her size and the extent of her injuries:

- To lift a small kitten, cup her body in your palm and use your other hand to prevent her from rising or bouncing away (by petting her or applying slight downward pressure). If the kitten is fighting you, it may be necessary to scruff her neck (as her own mother would) but support her hind legs so that she does not dangle or swing about.

- To lift an adult cat, place one arm along the length of her abdomen and chest and cradle her body close to yours. Grasp both her front legs between the fingers of your hand to prevent her from breaking free or from scratching you. With your other hand, hold your cat's head and neck close to you to give her a sense of security in your arms. Some cats are better carried tucked under your arm and held close to you by pressing the cat's body between your arm and your side, especially if they are fighting against you.

To lift an agitated or aggressive cat, scruff the neck and hold the cat with the paws facing away from you. Use your other hand to grasp the back legs and support the cat's weight.

- Another way to lift a more agitated or aggressive cat is somewhat more severe but gives you a safer grip. Scruff the back of the cat's neck to lift and hold the cat with her paws facing away from you. With your other hand, support the cat's weight and grasp the back legs between your fingers to provide further control.

- It is often helpful to use a towel or pillow case to cover a struggling cat to minimize your own injury and to give her a comforting sense of being hidden from additional harm.

31

Reassure your cat as you lift and carry her. She may struggle to get free because of pain or panic. Keep your hold firm but do not grip tightly unless it is absolutely necessary to prevent further injury to yourself or your pet.

If your cat is unconscious or unable to walk, she may be suffering from serious internal injuries or head and spinal cord trauma. For these patients, (and for a very overweight cat that is too awkward or heavy to lift) it might be best to transport on a stretcher. Depending on the size and weight of your cat, you can use a box or even an open suitcase. If a piece of plywood or particle board is available, you could lift this alone but it would be better with the help of an assistant. You may also use the lid of a garbage can, a basket, a gym bag with a solid bottom, a desk drawer or anything else that is appropriate and available. Remember that the stretcher has to be small enough to fit into the car, so it may only be of use to transport to the vehicle. If you are unable to easily locate an item that could be used as stretcher, don't waste time constructing a

Almost anything can be used as a stretcher—for a small cat, a box can work just fine.

makeshift stretcher. It is far more important to get your cat to the nearest emergency facility as quickly as possible. More often than not, the easiest and best stretcher will be a jacket or coat, blanket or sheet, mat or area rug. Cover your injured cat with a blanket or any article of clothing to preserve body heat. Place your cat's back against the back of the car seat or even on the floor of your vehicle so that she will not be unnecessarily jostled during transport. Your pet already has enough problems without rolling off the car seat.

Drive carefully! Concentrate on traffic, road obstacles and the shortest route to your destination. Obviously, successful transportation of the patient to the emergency facility is a critical aspect of first aid. Don't forget to breathe! Continue speaking to your cat in a calm and soothing voice while you drive.

How to Give Medication

Medicating a sick or injured cat can be one of the greatest challenges of pet ownership. Somehow, even the most passive and gentle cat can become downright ornery when it comes to being medicated or manipulated in order to receive medication. The administration of prescribed drugs can be important in preventing emergencies. For example, your cat may be on a course of prescribed drugs to treat a serious illness. Although the administration of medication will rarely be required of the cat owner in an emergency, you might be instructed to do so by your veterinarian.

> **KEEPING CALM WILL SOOTHE YOUR CAT**
>
> If your cat is injured, remain calm and speak softly to your cat to reassure her. Even if a cat does not seem badly injured, she will be in a state of high anxiety and could progress into a state of shock. Avoid making sudden movements or rushing toward your cat. Instead, keep your arms relaxed and your facial expression as neutral as possible. Your cat is always attuned to your verbal cues, facial expressions and body language and will be even more responsive in a crisis.

HOW TO GIVE ORAL MEDICATION

Medicines that are taken by mouth (oral) come in tablet (chewable or nonchewable), capsule, gel capsule and liquid forms.

To administer medication in pill form (tablet or capsule) directly into the cat's mouth:

1. Place your cat in your lap or atop an elevated surface.

2. Encircle the top of your cat's head with one hand between your thumb and fingers.

3. Gently elevate the head so that her nose is pointing upward; in this position, the lower jaw will drop down slightly.

4. With your other hand, use your pinkie finger to gently press downward on the lower jaw and quickly drop the tablet or capsule to the very back of the tongue so that the medication is more likely to be

swallowed. If you are very quick, use your index finger to push the pill deeper into the throat and quickly withdraw your hands and release your cat.

5. If you are unsure whether your cat has swallowed the medicine, release the cat's lower jaw but maintain your hold on her head and slide your thumb under her jaw to gently hold the mouth closed with your fingers. To encourage swallowing, gently rub her nose with a finger (she will swallow and try to lick her nose) or blow gently onto her nose to tickle it (this will also stimulate swallowing and licking her nose). Rubbing her throat may also be effective to trigger the swallowing reflex.

6. Release your cat after you see her swallow, but observe her for a few moments before you assume you have been successful. Some animals can become very adept at holding onto a pill without swallowing it. Be sure the medication is introduced far back on the tongue so that this trick is less successful.

CHECK WITH YOUR VETERINARIAN BEFORE GIVING MEDICATION

Never administer any kind of medication or treatment to your cat without first consulting your veterinarian. Do not assume that a remedy that has been recommended in the past for a particular symptom will again be appropriate should the same or similar symptoms recur. Many medical conditions resemble one another, but their treatments may be very different. An accurate diagnosis must be made. You should not guess at what treatment is right for your pet without your veterinarian's input.

To give a tablet or capsule, it is generally not recommended to crush the medicine in food. Most drugs have an unpleasant taste that could be released when the pill's coating is unsealed.

If you are unable to give a pill directly into your cat's mouth by the method described above, you may need to hide it in food or a treat. Always be sure that the tablet or capsule has been swallowed. Your cat might eat around the pill and leave it in her dish or carry the pill elsewhere and then spit it out. For that reason it is preferred to hide the medication in a small portion of food (a piece of soft cheese, peanut butter, luncheon meat or any favorite food item that is just large enough to cover the pill) and stay to watch as your cat consumes the treat and its hidden "cargo." Similarly, you

can dip the tablet in margarine or butter to help lubricate its passage and hide the taste when you follow the
directions for pilling your cat outlined above. Another
tip is to freeze the pills with a ¹/₄ teaspoon of water or
broth; these will slide easily past the tongue and down
the hatch and if tasted, won't be unpleasant!

Some solid oral medications are prepared as chewable
tablets that are specially flavored to appeal to your cat.
Most cats find these tablets very palatable, but if your
cat refuses them, mix the chewable tablet with the cat's
food or favorite treat as discussed above.

To administer liquid oral medication, gently place the
dropper at the corner of the cat's mouth where the top
and bottom lips meet. Deliver the liquid onto the back
of the tongue by placing the tip of the dropper
between the back teeth. If your cat resents the flavor of
the liquid medication (spits up, drools heavily or foams
at the mouth), you could try mixing it into her food or
hiding it in a special food treat or frozen treat as
described above.

If you need to give your cat medicine, it is best to hide it in a morsel and hand-feed your cat her "treat." Taking medicine will become a fun activity for you both!

Avoid giving oral medication far back in the throat
with the head elevated in line with the neck. This pos-
ture increases the risk of aspirating the liquid or tablet
(inhaling into the lungs). A 45-degree angle of eleva-
tion is safe, effective and need not be exceeded.

If your veterinarian has instructed you to remove food and/or water from your cat, do not administer medication in food treats as described above unless you consult with your cat's veterinarian.

If you have difficulty medicating your cat despite great efforts, do not hesitate to seek help from someone at your veterinary clinic. Gadgets commonly known as "pill poppers" are available through your veterinarian and can be very helpful. Unfortunately, some cats can be very determined and refuse any attempt to be medicated or treated. In fact, some can become aggressive or unintentionally injure their owners during attempts to treat them. In this case, you may be required to bring your pet to the clinic for her daily treatment, or an alternative medication or route of administration (e.g. injectable) may be advised. It might be necessary to hospitalize or board your cat at the clinic until all the necessary treatments have been completed.

How to Give Eye Medication

Eye (ophthalmic) medications come in liquid or ointment form. Eye drops may be slightly easier to apply than ointments because they can be delivered more quickly. However, some cats feel uncomfortable when they feel the drop fall onto the surface of the eye. Ointments may take a bit more control to deliver to the eye but may, in some instances, remain in the eye longer for greater benefit in healing. Discuss the advantages and disadvantages of a liquid or ointment ophthalmic medication with your veterinarian in case the drug he or she has chosen is available in both forms. Ask someone at home to help hold your cat if she squirms or resists your attempts to medicate her eyes. Wrap her in a towel with only her head exposed to protect yourself from being scratched.

To administer ophthalmic drops/ointment to your cat:

1. Encircle her head in your hand and use your fingers to slide the skin of the upper eyelid toward the top of the head; your cat will naturally move her eye downward and away from you.

2. With your other hand, hold the medication bottle or tube and rest the side of your palm on the side of your cat's face, just off to the side of the eye being medicated (this will also help to steady the cat's face to minimize further injury to the eye in case she struggles).

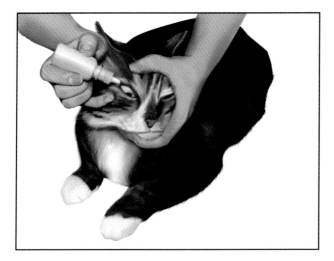

Eye medication comes in drops or ointment and should be introduced from the corner of the cat's eye.

3. Instill the required number of drops or the recommended amount of ointment onto the outside corner of the eye's surface and release the upper eyelid as you allow the eyelids to gently blink.

You may want to give your cat a pea-sized treat as a reward for her tolerance of your manipulation. A treat might increase her patience with you when the next treatment is due!

HOW TO GIVE EAR MEDICATION

Ear (otic) medication is available in liquid and ointment form. Your veterinarian will prescribe the medication that is appropriate for your cat's ear problem. An ear culture may be necessary but might not be suggested unless your cat's ears do not respond to the first medication selected for use. Treatments might be easier if you place your cat on your lap or a chair. It is sometimes necessary to roll a towel around her body so that only her head is exposed to facilitate medication and minimize your risk of being scratched.

To administer otic medication to your cat:

1. Grasp the ear between your thumb and a bent index finger (to avoid pinching the ear do not use your fingertip) and visually locate the entrance to the ear canal. Most ear infections originate deep inside the ear canal, and medication must be instilled directly into the canal to be effective.

2. Gently place the nozzle of the tube or bottle as deep as possible into the canal (these containers are designed to deliver otic medications into the cat's ear canal) and instill the recommended dosage of medication. You will not injure your cat's ear because the canal turns at a right angle and the container tip cannot reach the eardrum. Do not release your hold on the ear until you are done!

Lift the ear to view the ear's internal structures and to visualize the entrance to the ear canal.

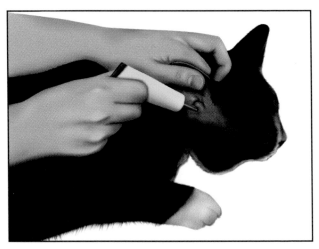

3. Release the ear but hold your cat's head while you gently massage the base of her ear to help distribute the medication inside the ear canal (you will hear it squishing inside her ear).

Unless your cat is on a rigid diet, give her a tiny but tasty treat as a reward for her patience and tolerance of your manipulation. It may facilitate the next treatment!

How to Give CPR

Cardiopulmonary resuscitation (CPR) is the popular name given to two distinct emergency procedures: 1) artificial respiration, which allows oxygen to be delivered when breathing has stopped, and 2) heart massage (cardiac massage), which maintains blood flow when the heart has ceased to beat on its own. In many cases, breathing and heartbeat will stop together and both artificial respiration as well as heart massage will be necessary, but this is not always so. Sometimes, the heart will continue to beat (for a few minutes) even when respiration has stopped and breathing may continue briefly when the heart has arrested. It is, therefore, important to determine three things before CPR is attempted:

1. Make sure that the patient is unconscious. You do not want to perform CPR on an animal that does not need it or that might bite you if you try to breathe into her nose unnecessarily. Call the cat's name loudly, clap your hands above her head, rub your knuckles across her ribs, pinch (hard if necessary) the skin between the toes to see if she pulls her paw away. If the cat responds to any of the above, delay performing CPR.

2. Verify the presence or absence of a heartbeat. The beating heart will be felt most strongly on the left side of the chest just behind the bent elbow, but it can also be detected on the right side of the chest. Place your palm over the cat's chest and press down slightly for better contact with the heartbeat (this will be especially important with cats that have a thick coat or are very overweight). You may also verify the capillary refill of the gums or check for a pulse in the neck (carotid artery) or inside the leg (femoral artery). Determining that the heart is beating, however, is a far more reliable test in an emergency.

3. Verify the presence or absence of breathing. Watch for even a faint movement of the ribs (place your hands lightly on the cat's chest wall if you are

unsure of what you see). Put your hands just in front of the nostrils to detect warm air as it is expelled.

Note: If either artificial respiration or cardiac massage or both are required, call for help and transport your cat immediately to the nearest veterinary clinic. If possible, call ahead to notify the veterinary staff of the nature of your emergency and approximately when you will arrive.

To give artificial respiration:

1. Make sure that the cat is unconscious and not breathing as described above.

2. Place the cat on her right side. (Should you need to administer cardiac massage, the left side of the chest will already be accessible—an important exception to this is when there is an obvious chest wound on the left side. In this case, place the cat on her left side, despite the injury, so that the healthy lung on the right side is free to breathe more easily.)

3. Examine the mouth and back of the throat to remove any foreign matter that could be blocking the airway or that might fall into the airway when you begin artificial respiration. If the unconscious cat is not breathing and her chest does not inflate when you begin artificial respiration, check the inside of the mouth and throat. Open the mouth by parting the upper and lower jaws. Pull the tip of the tongue forward and downward toward the cat's chest to dislodge any obstructing material and to get a clear view. Scoop away solid debris and wipe any heavy mucus, saliva, blood, vomit or foreign object that may be found. If necessary, reach with your finger into the back of the cat's throat to feel for any obstructing object or material. If you see an object but cannot reach it, use a spoon or tweezers (do not to push it farther into the airway!); begin CPR immediately following removal of the obstruction.

4. Encircle the cat's muzzle with one hand and support her neck with your other hand (avoid unnatural neck positions that could interfere with the flow of air or aggravate any hidden injury).

5. Keeping the mouth closed firmly, place your mouth over the cat's nose and exhale deeply but without real force (like blowing out several candles at once for artificial breathing into an adult cat, and like one candle for a kitten's respiration) for about one to two seconds to bring about a moderate rise of the patient's rib cage, signaling adequate inflation of the lungs.

6. Remove your mouth from the cat's nose to allow the lungs to deflate and the cat to exhale (do not let go of the muzzle; keep your face close to the cat for efficient technique but your eyes on the patient's chest to monitor the rise and fall of the rib cage and lungs).

7. Repeat each assisted breath every two seconds.

8. Check for the presence of a heartbeat at least three times every minute by placing one hand on the chest wall just behind the cat's bent left elbow. If there is no heartbeat, you will need to begin heart massage as described below. To avoid permanent brain injury, do not stop artificial respiration for longer than thirty seconds; continue CPR during transport, as needed.

Note: If the cat's gum color does not return to a more normal pink, or if the chest does not rise or fall when you perform artificial respiration, the airway may be obstructed. In an effort to expel whatever solid or liquid matter might be obstructing the flow of air, suspend the cat upside down by holding each thigh in one hand or by encircling her hips; swing her from side to side in a wide arc. Repeat the swing method as necessary or, with the palms of your hands, compress and release the middle of each side of her chest at the level of the last ribs; (the chances of reviving the cat are, unfortunately, very remote if there is a deep airway obstruction). Check the mouth and throat again to

Fundamentals
of First Aid

remove or wipe away anything that has been expelled and return to artificial respiration.

If the cat coughs or seems to move in any way, suspend your CPR and check to see if she has begun to breathe independently and if the heartbeat is present. *Do not continue CPR if the cat is breathing and the heart is beating.* Observe your patient for any changes in case you need to resume resuscitation and transport to the nearest veterinary clinic *immediately*.

To give cardiac massage:

Once your cat is breathing independently, observe her for any respiratory changes in case you need to resume CPR.

1. Place the cat on her right side, with the left side facing up, as the base of the heart is closest to the surface in this position. If the cat has an obvious injury to the right side of the chest, place the cat on her left side (cardiac massage might be a bit less efficient to the right side of the chest, but you need not risk puncturing a lung or the heart with broken ribs during CPR!).

An alternative position for very obese cats or those with obvious chest injuries requires the cat to be placed slightly on her back; place one hand on either side of the cat's chest about ⅓ of the way between the sternum and the elbow. Compress the chest between both your hands (see below).

2. If possible, elevate the cat's hips to facilitate the flow of blood returning to the brain and vital organs.

3. For small- and medium-sized cats, place your thumb and fingers on either side of the chest just behind and slightly below the bent elbow. For very large or very obese pets, place the heel of one hand just behind and slightly below the bent elbow. Use two fingers for very young kittens.

4. Compress the chest wall over the heart and release between each compression without removing your hand (press just enough to depress the chest lightly) at a rate of 120 compressions per minute (count out loud to help keep the rhythm: "1-and-2-and-3-and-4-and-5-and-1-and-2-and-3-and-4-and-10-and-1-and-2-and-3-and-4-and-15"; compress on each digit, release on "and"). Do not worry about pressing too hard but on the other hand avoid compressing the chest too roughly; think of the action of jumping up and down on a trampoline.

5. If you are alone and both artificial resuscitation and cardiac massage are required (unassisted CPR), perform one quick breath after every five cardiac compressions. For greater efficiency, keep one hand on your patient's head and your head close to her face as you continue chest compressions between respirations.

If you have an assistant, one person should perform artificial resuscitation and the other should perform cardiac massage; synchronize your efforts at a rate of one breath per three to five compressions.

Stop CPR every three to five minutes (or before if any movement is detected) to check for the presence of a pulse or heartbeat and for independent respiration. If the cat's pupils remain fixed and dilated despite CPR, a good prognosis (final outcome) is unlikely.

As mentioned above, do not stop artificial respiration for longer than thirty seconds to avoid permanent brain injury; continue performing CPR during transport as needed.

Note: If artificial respiration and/or cardiac massage are required, call for help and transport your pet immediately to the nearest veterinary clinic. Call ahead, whenever possible, to notify the veterinary staff of the nature of your emergency and approximately when you will arrive.

Addressing

part two

Emergencies

chapter 3

External

Wounds

External problems in your cat can range from an ingrown nail to an infected bite wound from another cat. Regardless of the problem's severity, you will want to address it quickly and properly.

Abscesses

If you find a local swelling of any size on your cat, it could be an abscess but it could also be a tumor, cyst, insect bite, hematoma (pocket of blood caused by blunt trauma), fracture, or soft tissue trauma (sprain, pocket of fluid). To distinguish these maladies from an abscess, you should know that:

- an abscess will usually be warm or even hot to the touch
- touching the swelling may be painful to the cat (be careful not to antagonize an injured cat)

- your cat may have an elevated body temperature (103°F or higher) or he may have a normal temperature

- your cat may withdraw socially and stop eating or he may behave normally in every way

- breaks in the skin (bite, scratch, puncture, insect stinger and the like) near or at the swelling site usually indicate the route of bacterial invasion

- a maturing abscess that is close to rupturing will have a softer spot (or several areas of uneven consistency) where surface rupture is likely

- recent conflict with another animal increases the likelihood that the swelling is an abscess even if an injury is unnoticeable at first.

An abscess can occur anywhere on the body. Sometimes, the source of the infection is not external (from an injury) but internal (from inside the body). The most common example is from a tooth root abscess of the upper row of teeth, which produces a characteristic abscess on the cheek below the eye. The treatment for a tooth root abscess includes draining the abscess, appropriate antibiotics and dental extraction by your veterinarian.

The anal glands or sacs, scent-marking organs located on either side of the cat's anus, can occasionally become impacted and infected. Infected anal glands (anal sacculitis) can rupture at or near the anus and are painful and sometimes complicated to heal. Anal glands should be examined by your veterinarian if your cat is chewing at his backside, scooting his rump along the ground, biting at his tail or seems to be uncomfortable when you approach his tail. Disinfection, antibiotics and, rarely, surgical excision of the infected sacs may be included in your cat's treatment.

> ### IF YOUR CAT HAS A FEVER
>
> If your pet has a fever, do not give him any aspirin or other medication that might mask the fever. The fever response is an adaptive defense mechanism that benefits your cat and, in most cases, you should not interfere. The problem is not the fever—the problem is the infection.

If your pet has a swelling on his body surface that might be an abscess, you should *schedule a veterinary visit within twenty-four hours.* In the interim, an ice pack placed at the site may provide some relief. Take the cat's rectal temperature to make sure that it is normal. If the temperature is elevated, your veterinarian will want to see your cat the same day to expedite treatment. Do not feed your cat the day of your veterinary visit in case he requires surgical drainage on the same day. Any wound infested with maggots (fly larva) should receive immediate attention. These immature insects burrow deep into the cat's skin and create complicated wounds and much misery. Please do not delay veterinary attention.

Always wear examination gloves when treating infected wounds or sores.

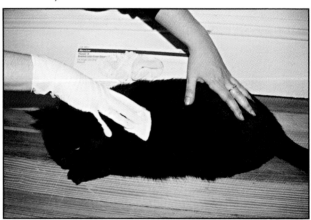

If the abscess has already begun to drain pus:

1. Do not touch it with your bare hands! Put on latex exam gloves, dishwashing gloves or any type of clean glove that you can wash later.

2. If your cat tolerates it and if you have the stomach for it, wipe the pus away with a paper towel, and press gently on the abscess to encourage further drainage from the open wound.

3. Pour lukewarm water into the wound to flush out additional infected material and debris.

4. Additional flushing with hydrogen peroxide may be helpful, once most of the pus is out of the cavity of the abscess.

5. Cover with a clean dressing and secure with a bandage (see chapter 2).

6. Call your veterinarian for an appointment *the same day.*

Laceration

A laceration is a cut. Lacerations can be minor and superficial or they can be deep and severe. Superficial cuts can bleed profusely and long gaping wounds can produce minimal bleeding. Refer to the discussions in chapter 2 on disinfecting wounds, making a bandage and bleeding for additional details.

If the cut is superficial and relatively small (less than 1 inch long), cover the wound with a clean or sterile gauze or paper towel and apply direct manual pressure for at least five minutes to stop the bleeding. Ideally, place an ice pack over the dressing and apply direct manual pressure. If the bleeding continues when you release pressure, resume pressure for an additional five to ten minutes before releasing. Sprinkle about 1 teaspoon of sodium bicarbonate onto the wound and continue to apply direct pressure (with ice). If a small cut continues bleeding for more than fifteen minutes, call your veterinarian to be seen right away.

> **WOUNDS OF UNKNOWN ORIGIN**
>
> If you do not know how your pet was originally wounded or if it was due to contact with another animal of any kind, there is a small but significant risk of contact with the rabies virus. This virus causes a fatal disease in all mammals, including people, and is transmitted through contact with any bodily fluid. Avoid direct contact with any open wound and seek veterinary attention for your cat without delay. In addition to any treatments necessary for the wound, a rabies vaccination booster may be necessary (even if your cat has had one recently) and your veterinarian will advise you on any quarantine period that is required by law in your area. Keep all your pet's vaccinations, including the rabies vaccine, current throughout his lifetime.

If bleeding has stopped or was never significant, pour soapy lukewarm water over the wound and follow with clear lukewarm water to flush away any superficial debris. Pat or blot dry—rubbing the surface may disturb blood clots and bleeding could resume. Apply a topical antibiotic ointment (from your first aid kit) and apply a bandage or light dressing. Keep the bandage clean and dry and change the bandage and dressing on a daily basis. If the wound seems to be clean and dry, simply reapply the ointment. However, if you see any sign of redness surrounding the cut, any discharge resembling pus or if the wound remains open after several days, flush with hydrogen peroxide and pat dry before reapplying the ointment and dressing. If there is no improvement after three to five days, if the wound causes the animal pain or if a fever develops, you should schedule a veterinary visit as soon as possible for additional treatment.

If the wound is greater than 1 inch long and cuts deeply into the skin's layers or deeper still into subcutaneous or muscular layers, cover the wound with a clean or sterile gauze, paper towel or towel and apply direct pressure to stop the bleeding. Use an ice pack to complement the effects of manual pressure; do not release your pressure for a full ten minutes. Gently pour soapy lukewarm water over the wound and follow with clear lukewarm water to flush away any superficial debris (do not rub the surface, pat it dry). Apply a bandage or light dressing, and call the veterinary hospital to advise them that you are on the way in with an emergency laceration.

If a laceration bleeds profusely around your hands during manual pressure and shows no sign of slowing down after five minutes, *do not release your pressure. Note:* bleeding from the ears, feet or tail is often messy and although these injuries require professional care they are not fatal; uncontrolled bleeding elsewhere deserves immediate veterinary attention. Transport your cat to the nearest clinic *immediately.*

If the wound is on the tail or a limb, try applying direct manual pressure to the major supply vessels closer to the body (elevate the tail/limb if possible):

- tail—press your fingers along the midline groove that runs the length of the underside of the tail to compress the major supply vessels
- front leg—wrap your hand around the leg and squeeze tightly about halfway to the shoulder or

just above the elbow (depending on where the cut is located and which seems to help more)

- rear leg—wrap your hand around the lower leg and squeeze tightly if the injury is below this level; for leg injuries above the knee, major supply vessels are located on the inside of the thigh about one-third of the way between the front and back of the leg; apply pressure to the inside of the leg with flattened fingers.

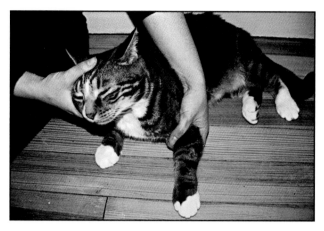

For a front leg injury, apply direct manual pressure by wrapping your hand around the leg above the injury.

If the wound is on a tail or limb and direct manual pressure to the major vessels fails, apply a tourniquet (discussed below) above the laceration site; gradually tighten the tourniquet until bleeding stops or at least slows down. Tourniquets are a last resort and can cause permanent injury if left on too long, but in an emergency, the risk is worthwhile. Transport your cat immediately to the nearest veterinary facility. Remain calm and keep your pet calm to minimize further blood loss.

If a laceration of any size starts to bleed again despite your efforts, resume direct pressure with any clean dressing or towel and proceed directly to the nearest veterinary facility.

APPLYING TOURNIQUETS

A tourniquet is any device that compresses a blood vessel to stop the bleeding of a tail or limb. As a last resort, apply a tourniquet for uncontrolled bleeding prior to and/or during transport to the hospital. The force exerted by a tourniquet is stronger than manual pressure alone. They should be used only when direct manual pressure and ice fail. Tourniquets can cause permanent injury if left on for longer than absolutely necessary although, in an emergency, the benefits far outweigh any risk.

If the wound is relatively small, place the tourniquet directly over a thick dressing. If the wound is larger, if there is no dressing or if bleeding continues despite a tourniquet applied directly over the injured site, try placing the tourniquet 2 or 3 inches closer to the body. *Note:* In this position and if the tourniquet successfully stops the flow of blood, a light dressing can be placed over the wound, but do not delay unnecessarily before seeking emergency treatment.

The simplest type of tourniquet can be made with bandaging material or a strip of cloth. Place a thick dressing of gauze squares, cloth or even a clean sanitary pad over the wound. Tie the tourniquet around the bleeding wound, or slightly above it if necessary, and tighten the knot until bleeding slows or stops completely.

Here is another way to fashion a tourniquet:

1. Tie a knot with the bandage or cloth strip over the injury or slightly above it.
2. Place a stick, spoon, pen or pencil over the first knot and tie a second knot around the object.
3. Tighten the knot and twist the stick-like object you have chosen until bleeding is controlled.
4. Lay the object parallel to the tail or limb and wrap in place with bandaging material.

Tourniquets are not comfortable for the victim (if he is conscious). This is no time to worry about hurting your cat. Your decision to apply a tourniquet was made because of uncontrolled hemorrhage. Transport *immediately.*

For a detailed discussion of how to dress a bleeding wound and how to apply bandages and splints, see chapter 2.

Scratches and Punctures

SCRATCHES

A scratch (abrasion) can be caused by conflicts with other animals but can also occur by contact with abrasive or jagged surfaces, such as rocks or certain plants. Superficial scratches generally require only light disinfection of the skin. For deep scratches, however, it is advisable to clip the hair to promote healing. Keep the wound clean and dry. Apply an antibiotic ointment two to three times per day for at least seven days. It is usually not necessary to cover the wound with a dressing. Always watch for any signs of infection, such as redness, swelling, local heat, fever, pain or discharge (pus).

A scratch can result from contact with rough outdoor surfaces.

PUNCTURES

A puncture wound can be defined as any perforating injury that is deeper than it is wide. A puncture wound may be linear or circular. Puncture wounds may be the result of being bitten. A bite wound often has at least two puncture wounds that correspond to the upper canine teeth of the aggressor, but there may be only one puncture wound caused by a bite if only one tooth made contact. Punctures may also be due to other causes, such as trauma from a knife or gunshot. A knife wound, for example, will cause a linear puncture (or stab wound). A bullet wound is generally circular at the point of entry and can be quite small depending on the bullet caliber. If there is an exit wound, it may be much larger and have irregular borders. Punctures can

53

also result from a fall on a perforating object, such as a pointed stick, a pitchfork, a shard of broken glass or metal fragment. If your cat has a puncture wound, there may be much bleeding or very little depending on the location of the injury, the tissues that were damaged and the cause of injury. In the event of a puncture wound, you should:

- Evaluate the whole animal; is he agitated or is he unusually calm? Is the cat conscious or unresponsive? Can you find a heartbeat? Is the cat breathing?

- Look for signs of shock (see chapter 2), such as pale or pasty gums and a rapid pulse. Perform CPR as necessary; keep your pet warm; do not focus on disinfecting the wound or taking your cat's temperature; that can be done later when the patient is stable.

- If there is profuse bleeding, apply direct pressure to the site or a pressure bandage and transport your cat to the nearest veterinary facility.

- If the wound penetrates the chest, a lung may have been punctured (hold your hand over the injury to feel for the passage of air that coincides with exhaling), major vessels may have been severed, or the heart itself may have been lacerated. If necessary, press a clean or sterile dressing directly into the open wound to fill the space. Transport to the nearest veterinary clinic *immediately.*

- If the perforating object has remained embedded in your cat, *do not remove the object!* The object itself may be controlling bleeding in deeper tissues by pressure against blood vessels. Moreover, by withdrawing the object you may cause additional damage and pain to your cat. Keep your cat warm and calm; transport him *immediately* to the nearest veterinary clinic (call ahead if you can so your cat can have immediate attention and treatment).

Whenever your cat is wounded, get as much information as possible about the circumstances surrounding the injury. The details could be important to help your veterinarian provide the appropriate treatments. For example, if another animal caused the wound, a rabies vaccine booster may be required, or if a rusty nail caused it a tetanus antitoxin may be advisable.

Burns and Scalds

Burns can be caused by electrical cords or outlets, heat or fire, hot grease or oil, inhaled smoke and many corrosive chemicals. Scalds are caused by hot or boiling liquids, most typically hot water or spilled food items from the stove top or the oven. There are two major criteria used to evaluate the severity of these injuries:

Train your cat at a young age to stay off the stove and kitchen counters.

1. The percentage of the body surface that was damaged, and

2. the depth of the burn:

   • first degree—superficial: Pain, redness, blistering may occur; the hair may be singed but hair follicles remain firm; healing is usually uneventful and rapid

   • second degree—moderate: Pain, redness, blistering are evident; the hair may remain firm; healing will be gradual

   • third degree—severe: All layers of skin are destroyed, leaving a black or pearly white wound; the hair is destroyed—initially, there may be little or no pain; healing will leave serious scars unless plastic surgery is performed.

First-degree burns that cover a small area (such as $\frac{1}{2}$ square inch) usually require only basic first aid. If the sore starts to look moist, becomes very itchy or still looks red after two or three days, it should be seen by your veterinarian. Second- or third-degree burns can be fatal, followed by shock, dehydration, or infection.

55

Depending on the severity of the injury, complications can be immediate or they can be delayed. Administer first aid and seek immediate veterinary attention.

First aid for very recent and minor first- or second-degree burns or scalds:

1. Pour cool water over the burned area (use a garden hose, kitchen sink, cold shower) or apply an ice pack for at least twenty minutes.

2. Blot the area dry with a clean and dry cloth (do not use a material that will leave lint or other particles that could adhere to the sore area).

3. Snip the hair from the wound surface and a 1-inch margin around it using the tip of a blunt scissors or a hair clipper intended for use on pets.

4. Apply topical antibiotic ointment.

5. If your cat tries to lick the wound, place a sterile non-stick dressing and a light bandage to cover the area. Change the dressing twice daily to keep the skin dry; watch for any signs of infection, such as redness, swelling, local heat, fever, pain or discharge (pus). See your veterinarian at the first sign of any delay in healing.

First aid for wide areas of first- or second-degree burns or scalds and for any size third-degree burn:

1. Check for signs of shock (see chapter 2). Keep your cat calm and cover him with a blanket if he is shivering.

2. If your cat shows no signs of shock (alert, completely normal behavior, gums pink, no difficulty breathing) apply a cool compress or ice pack to the injury for twenty minutes before seeking immediate veterinary care.

3. If your cat is showing signs of shock, seek veterinary care without delay.

First aid for chemical burns from an irritating or poisonous substance:

1. Protect your own skin with rubber or latex gloves (or any other glove that may be available) before you touch your cat; discard the gloves before touching anything else.

2. Remove and discard any collar, harness, bandanna or leash that could have been contaminated by the offending substance.

3. Wash your cat by repeatedly flushing with generous amounts of clear water (use a garden hose with a gentle stream of water or use your tub or shower).

4. Follow the water rinse with a bath using a liquid detergent (for hands or dish washing), work up a generous lather; rinse thoroughly and repeat.

5. Call your veterinarian's office for further instructions.

Your cat may burn or scald his mouth by licking a corrosive substance adhered to his coat (look for heavy drooling and unusual tongue movement), by electrocution due to chewing on an electric cord or simply by investigating a hot object, such as a frying pan, with his mouth.

First aid for an oral burn: Rinse the cat's mouth liberally and repeatedly with clear water. The oral cavity generally heals rapidly if you act quickly. If your cat has swallowed or licked a chemical compound, however, your next step should be to contact your veterinarian for further advice or to call the National Animal Poison Control Center at (800) 548-2428. Some substances are highly toxic even in minute quantities and your cat may require additional emergency care by a trained professional.

> **TO PREVENT BURNS AND SCALDS**
>
> Do not leave your cat, especially your kitten, unattended in a room with burning candles, lamps or any open flame, indoors or outdoors. Make sure that the screen to your fireplace is stable and that the door to your wood burning stove is secure. Keep pot handles facing inward on the stovetop or counter top and do not leave hot food items unguarded (especially on barbecues or grills) if your cat is prone to raiding for food. If you bathe your cat at home, use lukewarm (room temperature) water—test the water with your elbow before immersing him. Keep electrical cords covered so that they cannot be chewed. If cords cannot be rendered inaccessible, keep your cat out of that room.

Contact with Poison

Some poisons may be absorbed through the skin or mucous membranes. Poisons that may be ingested or inhaled are discussed in chapter 4. If your pet has been bitten by a snake or poisonous spider, apply an ice pack to the wound, keep your cat calm and take him to an emergency clinic right away. Try to recall the description of the snake or spider in detail to help your veterinarian decide what treatment will be best.

If your cat has come in contact (skin or hair) with an irritating or poisonous substance, protect your own skin with rubber or latex gloves (or any other glove that may be available) before you touch your cat. Remove any flea or tick collar that was placed on your cat's neck recently in case it is contributing to the problem. Wash your cat by repeatedly flushing with generous amounts of clear water (hose your cat down with a gentle stream of water in your yard/use your shower/fill the tub or sink to his mid-chest level and ladle water with a plastic or metal bowl or your hands, if necessary). Follow this by bathing him with a liquid detergent (for hands or dish washing), work up a generous lather, rinse thoroughly and repeat. Call the veterinary clinic to inform them of the nature of the substance that hurt your cat. Even if your cat seems fine after his bath, it may be wise to schedule an appointment to make sure everything is all right.

Allergic Reactions—Insect Bites and Stings

Allergy is a complex of extreme defensive reactions directed against external or internal allergy-causing substances or materials, collectively called allergens.

Allergic reactions are varied and can include itchiness, hives, facial swelling, red and tearing eyes, sinus congestion and sneezing, asthma, diarrhea and vomiting and other internal responses that can even be fatal. In clinical practice the treatment of allergy, for both people and other animals, involves:

- the identification of the allergen and its source
- the prevention of contact with allergens
- the control of allergic symptoms with specific medication.

When allergens are unavoidable (for example, when pollens fill the air beginning in the spring through the first frost in the northeastern United States) then controlled desensitization by a series of injections offers eventual relief to the allergy sufferer.

The control of mild to moderate allergic reaction is accomplished by the administration of antihistamines, which control the side effects of the allergic immune response. Your veterinarian may prescribe antihistamines to control your cat's allergy problems.

Your cat (and child) are susceptible to insect bites when outdoors, but only some will produce urgent situations.

There are many different antihistamines, and it is often a trial-and-error process to find the one that works best for your pet's symptoms. It should also be noted that an antihistamine may work well for a while and then lose its effectiveness, making it necessary to prescribe a different one. In cases where the allergic response has progressed to more considerable discomfort, other medications may be necessary.

Insects such as bees, wasps, hornets, flies, ants, ticks, fleas, spiders and mosquitoes can all leave their mark on your cat. Luckily, only a few will produce urgent situations. Most insect bites simply result in localized pain or itchiness. Removal of the insects with tweezers (e.g. tick) or pesticides (if your cat has fleas) and short-term management of related symptoms with antihistamine or corticosteroid are usually all that is required to resolve the problem.

Some spider bites, such as that of the black widow spider, trigger more than just a local allergic reaction.
The black widow delivers a poisonous bite that initially
will cause local pain and swelling before progressing to
generalized body pain, weakness and fever.

Bee stings are painful but a cat that is predisposed to
bee sting allergy could develop serious complications
to a second bee sting. The first time the cat is stung, he
may experience some local swelling or the reaction
may be so mild that it may go unnoticed. If the cat is
stung in the face, a common occurrence, then some
facial swelling may be obvious. Facial swelling can
progress to involve the upper airways and throat, however, and could obstruct the passage of air to the lungs.
Facial swelling is serious and warrants prompt first aid.

If you discover a swollen and itchy area on your cat's
skin, part the hair to see if you can detect a biting
insect, any obvious redness or the presence of a stinger
embedded in the skin. A bee stinger, for example,
looks like a very small (approximately ⅛ inch) fish-
hook and is easily removed with tweezers. Administer
6.25 to 12.5mg of diphenhydramine (Benadryl or its
generic equivalent) in tablet or liquid form. Keep this
over-the-counter medication on hand in your medicine cabinet and/or in your cat's first aid kit. Apply an
ice pack to the area to help control the itchiness and to
minimize swelling. Call your veterinary clinic to report
the incident, your cat's symptoms and current condition and to ask for further recommendations.

If you discover that your cat has a swollen muzzle and
puffy eyes, hives (skin swellings that resemble coins or
bumps) that are spreading over the cat's body and/or
severe itchiness anywhere on the body, you should
immediately administer 6.25 to 12.5mg of Benadryl (or
its generic equivalent diphenhydramine). It may take
as long as half an hour for the drug to begin its effect
and allergy-related symptoms may take up to half a day
to subside. Even if your cat seems to feel more comfortable shortly after antihistamine administration,
schedule a veterinary visit within twenty-four hours to
prevent any relapse and to plan on what to do if there

is another episode. When facial swelling is present, however, call your veterinarian right away and have your cat seen immediately, even if he doesn't seem bothered by his swollen face (which is unlikely).

Itchy Cat

A very itchy cat can lose sleep and weight, prevent his owner from sleeping, vocalize excessively, chew and scratch obsessively and even self-mutilate. Itchiness can come on gradually over many days or weeks or it can "explode" with little warning in its most intense form. If your cat is extremely itchy or uncomfortable (particularly if he is injuring himself because of this) then an itch is definitely an urgent symptom.

Use tweezers to remove ticks from your cat.

If your cat appears to be itchy, part his hair and investigate.

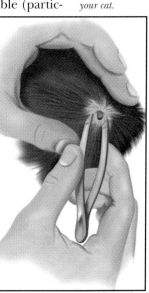

- Look for a tick—remove the tick with a pair of tweezers by firmly grasping its head as close to the cat's skin as possible. (Kill the insect by soaking it in alcohol or nail polish remover, or hold it up to a small flame so that it is dead before you discard it.)

- If you see a flea or black specks on the skin (these are flea feces and will stain reddish brown in a drop of water) treat your pet for flea infestation. Call your veterinary clinic for advice on current advances in flea and tick control.

- The skin may be red or blotchy, or you may find an infected sore, a puncture wound or a scratch. Clip the hair carefully with the tip of a blunt scissors and disinfect the area. Make an appointment for your cat to be seen at the first available opening.

- If you do not see any obvious explanation for your cat's discomfort, schedule a veterinary visit as soon as possible; bring a stool (fecal) sample with you in case it is called for (some internal parasites will make your pet feel itchy); additional laboratory tests may be advised.

- Note the area(s) where your cat is itchy, whether the discomfort has worsened since you first noticed it and exactly how long he has been uncomfortable so that you can relay important details to your veterinarian.

If your cat is more than just a little itchy, administer the antihistamine Benadryl (or its generic equivalent diphenhydramine) by mouth. Give 6.25 mg to kittens or small adults (under 5 pounds) and 12.5 mg to adult cats. You may repeat this every twelve hours, if neces-

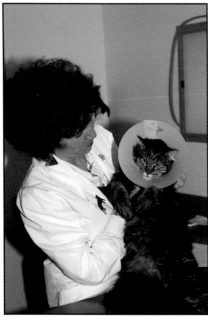

sary, until your veterinary visit; be sure to tell your veterinarian that you gave this medication to your cat and at which dose. When antihistamine alone does not ease your cat's distress, you may apply an ice pack to the itchy spot(s) for at least five minutes.

For extreme itchiness or if the itchiness is over a wide area or even generalized to the entire body, it may be necessary to prevent your cat from self-mutilation. An Elizabethan collar ("E collar," named for the fashionable wide collars worn in Elizabethan England) is intended to keep your cat from

An Elizabethan collar will keep your cat from licking or chewing himself from the neck down.

licking or chewing himself from the neck downward and from scratching or rubbing at his head. The height of the collar must be at least 1 or 2 inches longer than your cat's nose. You can fabricate an E collar by cutting a hole in a plastic flowerpot and tying it to your cat's collar with string. You can also make one with a wide strip of cardboard or plastic to fashion a cone-shaped collar around your cat's head. Alternatively, your veterinary clinic can supply a ready-made E collar until your scheduled appointment. Think of the E collar as damage control until your veterinarian can examine your cat and relieve any discomfort.

Paw Problems

A cat's foot is subject to a lot of abuse on a daily basis. Get your cat accustomed to having his feet and toes touched by gently manipulating these areas daily. Start when your cat is young—before an urgent problem develops. You may want to give your cat a small food treat to reward his tolerance of your probing between his toes, applying gentle pressure to his foot pads and feet and lifting each foot for examination. In case you need to examine the feet in an emergency or simply to trim his toenails, what an advantage you will have if your cat has been trained to tolerate this in advance!

If your pet has cut his paw, chances are there will be quite a bit of bleeding. The foot pads are highly vascularized (a high concentration of blood vessels). Apply direct pressure, or better yet, direct pressure with an ice pack. If bleeding continues or the cut appears deep, call your veterinarian to let him or her know that you need immediate attention. Continue direct pressure on the drive down or apply a pressure bandage. Do not panic, this is not a fatal injury, just a messy one!

If the cut seems superficial and bleeding is absent or easily controlled, flush the wound with lukewarm water. Follow with a five-minute foot soak in a small basin or bowl containing about ½ inch of water (enough to cover the injury) mixed with a capful of bleach. *Note:* The feet are very contaminated and easily become infected; bleach is a wonderful disinfectant and, although it may sting elsewhere on the body, its use is appropriate for the feet. Rinse again with clear water and pat the foot dry. Apply an antibiotic ointment, a dressing and a bandage. Change the bandage and dressing daily: Repeat the foot soak, flush with clear water and pat dry. Reapply the ointment before the clean dressing is applied.

You should arrange for a prompt veterinary visit if the cut produces a discharge resembling pus; fails to close; the borders and surrounding area become red; there is a lack of improvement after three to five days; pain or fever is present.

Swollen paws or toes may be caused by fractured bones, blunt trauma, soft tissue injury (such as torsion or sprains), infections, foreign bodies, insect bites, bandages that are too tightly applied or elastic bands that obstruct circulation. If your cat seems to be limping or licking at his feet:

1. Remove any bandage or dressing that was applied before the swelling was noticed and have your veterinarian reapply the bandage. If you applied the bandage yourself, make an appointment for the veterinarian to examine the paw.

2. Closely examine the cat's feet:

   • hold the paw, without squeezing or twisting it, and gently separate the toes to examine between them; gently press under each toe to exteriorize the claws for inspection; watch for broken, bleeding or infected toenails; do the same under the foot and examine each foot pad; look for any crack or cut on the foot pads or the skin between them

   • make sure there is no red, moist or swollen area or any unusual odor

   • use your fingers to double check for the presence of any penetrating splinter or foreign object, such as a sticky burr or insect stinger, which may be very small; remove what you find with tweezers.

3. If your cat's foot is causing him great pain or if you can see or feel "crunching in the foot," there may be fractured bones. Apply an ice pack, if possible, to minimize swelling and pain—bring your pet to the veterinarian the same day.

4. If you do not suspect a fracture and find only a small area of irritation (or nothing obvious at all) soak the foot in a basin or bowl of soapy lukewarm water, running your fingers between each toe and foot pad, and rinse thoroughly in clear water before patting dry. This will disinfect the foot

and, hopefully, remove any tiny splinters or insect barbs that remain undetected; also, any irritating substance on the skin or hair surface should be washed away.

5. If a toenail is broken or bleeding, flush debris by soaking in clear water and wrap in a non-stick dressing and bandage; have your cat seen within twenty-four hours.

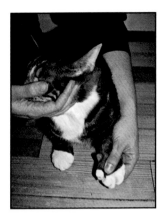

6. If there is no obvious reason for the licking or lameness, work your way up the cat's leg to search for any swelling or wound between the foot and the shoulder. If your cat seems otherwise unaffected (playful, eating well), schedule a veterinary appointment within twenty-four to forty-eight hours.

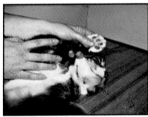

7. Regardless of whether you detect a problem, if your pet stops eating or is in real discomfort, see your veterinarian as soon as possible.

Gradually get your cat used to having his feet handled and his nails trimmed to prevent problems involving the toenails.

Sometimes sticky substances (like bubble gum, tree sap or tar) can adhere to the hair on a cat's feet or to foot pads (or anywhere else). Carefully snip the soiled hairs away with the tip of blunt scissors. Alternatively, hold an ice cube against the sticky stuff to make it harden—it will be easier to peel away.

INGROWN TOENAILS

A cat's toenails can grow long and curve downward to penetrate the foot pads. This is called an ingrown toenail. Cats manage the growth of nails by using scratch posts (e.g. a tree trunk outdoors, a scratching post inside) but sometimes, a nail can grow unexpectedly long. A cat's nails grow in length as well as in layers. The outer layers are shed when the cat scratches against a surface—this reveals a sharper nail beneath the old layers. Cats with "extra" toes (polydactyl cats) may have more problems than cats with the usual number of toes because the extra toenails are frequently hidden and hard to reach. Trimming your cat's nails is part of a good grooming habit and will greatly diminish the likelihood of the formation of ingrown nails and the serious infections and pain that result. It may be advisable to declaw the nail, particularly nails of polydactyl toes, which repeatedly cause problems.

A cat with arthritis in his feet may have twisted or deformed toes that do not place the toenail in an optimum position for wear. Toenails that have become ingrown are painful and have a high incidence of infection.

Accustom your cat to having his nails trimmed to prevent problems involving the toenails.

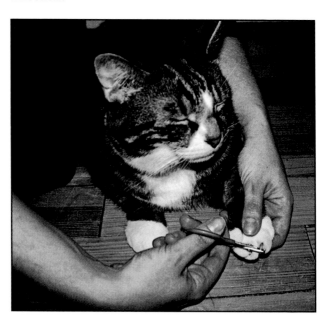

To treat ingrown toenails:

1. Trim the nail and pry it gently from the puncture wound it has created.

2. Disinfect with hydrogen peroxide (for foot injuries, diluted bleach is an acceptable alternative) on a cotton ball or gauze.

3. Apply a topical antibiotic.

4. It is usually unnecessary to apply a bandage unless the sore is open, but if your cat is licking at the site, cover it with a light dressing for two or three days; clean with disinfectant, reapply antibiotic ointment and replace the dressing daily.

5. If there continues to be any pus, foul smelling discharge, swelling, fever or discomfort after several days, see your veterinarian as soon as possible.

6. Keep your cat indoors at least until any wound, including ingrown toenails, is completely healed.

chapter 4

Internal Problems

Bowel Disorders
VOMITING

Vomiting is common in cats and frequently serves to rid the body of harmful substances. It is a nonspecific response to dozens of physical and emotional causes that frequently must be excluded, one by one, with laboratory testing and careful physical examination.

Vomiting can occur soon after swallowing an offending substance, or it can be delayed by many hours. Assist your veterinarian in making a diagnosis by reporting details that include how long after a meal did your cat vomit, how many times has she vomited in the last twenty-four hours, how many days has the vomiting continued and the appearance and contents of the vomited matter.

One of the most common reasons for vomiting in otherwise healthy cats is hairballs. During grooming, loose hairs are normally ingested and usually pass through the digestive system uneventfully. Hair can sometimes form solid plugs, however, that obstruct the intestine and cause vomiting. More often than not, the "hairballs" are expelled but they can also cause considerable gastrointestinal irritation or remain impacted. Hairballs may require surgical removal if the cat's vomiting is unable to dislodge the plug or if it does not pass with the stools.

Vomiting for any reason takes on more serious implications in very young kittens, cats older than 10 years of age and adult cats in poor health. Contact your veterinarian immediately if vomiting occurs in young, old or sick cats. For example, diabetic cats may need to decrease their daily insulin requirements or may need to be examined. Excessive vomiting can result in dehydration, electrolyte imbalance and, in extreme cases, shock. Seek professional advice within twenty-four hours if vomiting persists despite the suggestions that follow:

Hairballs are created when cats ingest hair following self grooming or grooming each other.

1. Measure your cat's rectal temperature. If it is higher than 103°F, call the clinic for an appointment the same day.

2. If the cat's temperature is within normal range, remove food and water (including treats) for twenty-four hours. If your cat has not vomited in the last eight hours you may give her a few teaspoons of water every few hours for the remainder of the fasting period, as long as she does not vomit. Do not be tempted to feed or give your cat water before the twenty-four hours are over, even if she

seems hungry and behaves normally, because you may precipitate more vomiting.

3. After twenty-four hours, place your cat on a bland diet consisting of boiled chicken or hamburger meat mixed with boiled or steamed white rice. Feed smaller and more frequent meals (three or four per day) of this special mix for two to three days before gradually reintroducing her regular food.

4. If vomiting resumes when food is reintroduced, remove food and water; call your veterinarian for further advice right away.

VOMITING AND HAIRBALLS

If your cat has only vomited once or twice and is otherwise behaving normally, she may have a problem passing a plug of hair, or a hairball, swallowed during grooming. Remove food and water for twenty-four hours. You may give her a petroleum jelly–based paste by placing little dabs of it on her nose or front leg (she will want to lick it off). Give ½ to 1 teaspoon once or twice a day for two to three days as long as she is not vomiting and is otherwise unaffected. If vomiting is due to hairball impaction, this remedy may help to lubricate its passage. If the vomiting is not due to a hairball, the remedy will not be harmful to the cat. If vomiting has ceased, resume feeding her after twenty-four hours with a bland diet and frequent meals (see description above). Mix the paste with her food for an additional day or two to ensure elimination of the hairball. You may not see it in her stools, but as long as she returns to normal you do not need to be concerned.

DIARRHEA

A bout of diarrhea (pasty or liquid stools) is not automatically an emergency. Diarrhea functions primarily to rid the digestive system of noxious contents. Diarrhea becomes a serious condition, however, if it is associated with fever, decreased appetite or vomiting or increasing lethargy. It is also of concern when the stools become very liquid, contain more than a drop of blood or if it continues for more than one or two days. Diarrhea can result in dehydration, electrolyte imbalance and, in extreme cases, shock. Call the clinic for an immediate appointment if you have any doubts about your pet's welfare. Bring a fecal sample, so that the veterinarian can check for the presence of internal parasites.

In kittens younger than 6 months of age, diarrhea can result in rapid decline. The younger the kitten, the more critical it is to obtain quick veterinary intervention. Do not delay your call for professional advice—your kitten should be seen the same day that the diarrhea appears.

Adult cats in poor health or cats over 10 years old should also be examined as soon as possible.

Regardless of your pet's age, if there is more than just a drop or two of blood or if the diarrhea is the color of dark chocolate or darker, call for an immediate veterinary visit.

If the diarrhea has not subsided (e.g. less frequent elimination, stools become firmer, cat seems more comfortable) within twenty-four hours of following the suggestions below, your pet should be seen by a veterinarian right away.

If your cat develops diarrhea but is otherwise unaffected:

- Place her on a bland diet consisting of boiled chicken or hamburger meat mixed with boiled or steamed rice.

- Feed smaller, more frequent meals (three or four per day) of this special mix until stools solidify and become normal.

- When bowel movements are firm, mix your cat's regular food with the bland diet for two or three more days before discontinuing the rice mixture.

71

- If you have any lingering concern, call your veterinarian to report the problem and describe your cat's current status in case your pet should still be seen. Ask if they would like you to bring in a fecal sample.

If your cat develops diarrhea but seems even slightly sluggish or if she is also vomiting, follow the plan outlined above as well as these additional suggestions:

- Measure your cat's rectal temperature (see chapter 2); if it is elevated (higher than 103°F), call the clinic for further advice.

- If the cat's temperature is normal, remove food and water (including treats) for twenty-four hours. If she has not vomited in the last eight hours you may give her a few teaspoons of water every few hours for the remainder of the fasting period, as long as she does not vomit. Reintroduce food by feeding a bland diet in small and frequent meals as described above.

- If vomiting and/or diarrhea resume when food is reintroduced, remove food and water; call your veterinarian for further advice.

CONSTIPATION

Constipation can be extremely uncomfortable for your cat. The absence of stools can be expected following a bout of diarrhea, for example, when bowel movements may be absent for a day or two. If the cat is eating and behaving normally, production should soon resume. Constipation is not an urgent symptom but should be considered serious if your pet has kidney disease, diabetes or any physical condition that predisposes her to dehydration. Also, if your cat is chronically constipated due to rectal dysfunction you will need to monitor stool production more closely. If apparent constipation is accompanied by vomiting or any sign of abdominal distress, have your cat examined by a veterinarian right away to be sure there is no intestinal obstruction.

If you see a piece of string, thread or ribbon protruding from the anus *do not pull it out!* This could lacerate the intestines and create a real emergency. Carefully trim the protruding filament to about ½ inch from the anus and, as long as your cat behaves normally, follow the home remedy for constipation below.

If stools are not produced for more than forty-eight hours:

- Add ½ to 1 teaspoon of a petroleum jelly–based paste mixed with food (you may use petroleum jelly available at your pharmacy or a prepared product prescribed by your veterinarian for hair-ball and constipation problems in cats). Alternatively, mix 1 to 2 teaspoons (depending on the size of your cat) of bran cereal into your cat's meals or one-fourth the adult dose of psyllium or Meta-mucil in her food.

If your cat becomes consti-pated, try mixing a little bran cereal or psyllium into her food.

- Encourage water intake as well as daily exercise. If bowel function does not resume normally within forty-eight hours, your cat should be examined and the choice of any additional treatment should be left to the professionals. *Do not administer laxatives or enemas to your cat without specific veterinary instruction.*

- If your constipated cat is also eating less than usual or not at all, she should be seen by a veterinarian without further delay.

73

Diabetic Emergencies

Insulin is a pancreatic hormone that is required in the metabolism of glucose, the major fuel used by the body's cells. Diabetes is a complex disease caused by an insufficient natural supply of insulin and requires cooperation between you and your veterinarian.

Without insulin, or when a confirmed diabetic fails to respond to insulin injection at the recommended dose, glucose levels rise in the blood stream and the resulting symptoms are associated with the body's attempts to adjust. Excessive thirst and excessive urination occur as the diabetic's body tries to dilute the concentration of glucose. Eventually, compensating mechanisms fail and deterioration, once begun, can be rapid.

Malaise and weight loss may be signs of uncontrolled diabetes.

When diabetes is diagnosed, insulin replacement therapy (by subcutaneous injection once or twice daily) is begun. With too high an insulin dose, the

blood glucose level may plummet. With its vital fuel supply devastated, the body collapses. The brain is the most sensitive organ to low blood glucose and thus tremors, seizure and the diabetic coma ensue.

If your cat drinks more than usual, urinates excessively, has a strange sweet smell to her breath, seems more subdued than usual and is losing weight, she may be an unconfirmed or uncontrolled diabetic. Schedule an appointment with your veterinarian to investigate further.

If your cat is diabetic, carefully follow your veterinarian's directions on how to fill the prescribed amount of insulin into the syringe and how to administer a subcutaneous injection. The most common reason that cats fail to respond to insulin injection is improper technique in administering the medication.

If your cat is a confirmed diabetic and is being regu-
lated with insulin injections, keep corn syrup or some
other form of liquid glucose on hand in case her blood
sugar drops. Because the body's metabolism is a dy-
namic process, blood sugar may drop even if the cor-
rect dose of insulin is administered.

Blood glucose will be at its lowest level approximately
four to eight hours after insulin administration,
although it may begin to drop sooner. To prevent glucose levels from plunging too rapidly, give your cat a
small meal about four to eight hours after insulin. If
your cat seems uncoordinated, confused, is shaking or
very sleepy four to eight hours after her insulin injection, her glucose levels may have dropped too low.

*Obesity in cats
makes it more
difficult to con-
trol diabetes.*

Give her about 1 teaspoon of sweet syrup directly
into her mouth, repeating
every fifteen minutes or so
until she seems more alert
and responsive. Feed her a
small meal of her regular
food and call your veterinarian right away for further
advice. If your cat is dazed
and unresponsive or loses
consciousness and cannot be
aroused (about four to eight

hours after insulin), rub 1 teaspoon of syrup directly
onto her gums; cover her with a blanket and take her to
the veterinarian *immediately.*

If your cat goes into convulsions four to eight hours
after insulin administration, very carefully lift her
upper lip and drizzle the teaspoon of syrup onto her
gums and release. Do not risk being bitten—your cat is
unconscious during a seizure and cannot control her
jaws. Cover her with a blanket and see your veterinarian *immediately.*

A diabetic cat who is vomiting, has diarrhea or has a
fever should be seen by a veterinarian within twenty-
four hours. In the interim, call the clinic for advice on
how to adjust the insulin dose before your scheduled
appointment.

Addressing
Emergencies

If you are late or miss giving your cat her scheduled injection, administer the recommended insulin dose and call the clinic for further directions.

Drug Sensitivities

Your cat may have a negative response to a medication prescribed to treat an unrelated illness. If she is on a course of medication and seems increasingly lethargic or unusually calm, stops eating, develops vomiting or diarrhea or starts to scratch/bite/rub herself, she may be showing signs of drug intolerance or sensitivity. Adverse drug reactions can develop with any medication, even a medication that was previously prescribed without incident, and suspected problems should be reported to your veterinarian without delay. *It is usually better not to discontinue a prescription without your veterinarian's instruction to do so.* Your veterinarian should be given the opportunity to determine whether the treatment is the cause of the problem or whether the underlying medical problem is failing to respond to the prescribed treatment. Call to make an appointment right away. Do not dismiss any concern you have regarding your cat's health.

> **DIABETES AND WEIGHT CONTROL**
>
> By maintaining your cat's ideal body weight, you will maximize her response to treatment. If she is obese, get advice on how to gradually reduce her weight to prevent diseases associated with obesity, such as diabetes. Add ½ to 1 teaspoon of bran cereal (depending on the size of your cat) to her food to help absorb some of the excess glucose in the intestine before it is absorbed. This should help to regulate your cat's glucose level, the amount of insulin needed and, as an added bonus, the regularity of bowel habits!

Note: Make certain that any suspected drug sensitivities are noted prominently on your cat's medical record. You should also keep a record of the drug name and the symptoms that developed from its use in case your cat is treated elsewhere and her file is unavailable for reference.

Urinary Problems

Urinary tract problems are diverse and include obstruction, infection, incontinence, inflammation, malformation and traumatic injuries, among many others. Sudden onset of kidney failure or complete urinary obstruction, for example, can have fatal consequences if left untreated. Fortunately, most urinary tract diseases are not immediately life-threatening, although they can be uncomfortable. Inflammation and/or infection of the feline bladder and urethra (feline lower urinary cat disease, FLUTD, previously called FUS, or feline urethral syndrome) may cause discomfort in females but can lead to fatal urinary obstruction in some males. Debris, blood clots or bladder crystals can plug the urethra as it narrows through the penis and can lead to blood toxicity and death within twenty-four hours. Always remember that an emergency should be defined in part by your cat's level of comfort and your own level of concern.

Signs of urinary tract problems include increased frequency, increased volume, straining to urinate and bloody urine.

Symptoms associated with urinary tract problems include:

- increased frequency of urination

- increased volume of urination

- pain during urination

- pink, brownish or reddish color of urine

- straining to urinate

- inability to pass urine

- increased frequency of drinking

- increased volume of water intake

- licking at penis or vulva (with or without discharge)

- inappropriate urination inside your home

Many of these same symptoms are common to several urinary ailments or are associated with problems that are unrelated to the urinary system. However, if any of these signs develop in your cat, she deserves veterinary attention within twenty-four hours. If your cat is straining to urinate, seems unable to urinate or has pain, see a veterinarian on the same day. If, in addition to any of these symptoms, your cat also has a fever, stops eating or drinking and becomes sluggish or withdrawn, see a veterinarian immediately. Whenever possible, try to collect a fresh urine specimen and, unless you leave within an hour or two, refrigerate it until you are on your way to the clinic. However, do not delay transport in an emergency in order to obtain a urine sample.

HOW TO COLLECT A URINE SPECIMEN

If your cat is used to using a litter box, empty all the litter filler. Clean the box thoroughly with diluted bleach and hot water; rinse and dry it completely. Confine your cat with the empty and disinfected box. She will probably urinate in it by the end of the day. Transfer the urine into a clean container and refrigerate until you deliver the specimen to the clinic (within twenty-four hours). If your cat refuses to use the box or ordinarily voids outdoors, consult with your veterinarian for further tips or instructions. In that case, it may be necessary to have the sample collected at the clinic.

Uterine and Vaginal Problems

The average female cat reaches sexual maturity by about 6 months of age. During cats' mating season, (from March through September), estrus ("heat") normally occurs every three weeks and usually lasts about one week, but each cat will develop her own pattern of estrus cycles. Your female cat, or queen, will not benefit, either behaviorally or physically, by coming into estrus even once, nor does she require the experience of producing a litter to lead a happy life. In fact, the opposite may be true. In addition to unwanted pregnancy and unnecessarily contributing to the tragedy of the homeless cat overpopulation, the physical consequences of keeping your cat intact are significant. Mammary tumors in cats (the equivalent of breast tumors in women), for example, are almost always very aggressive cancers. The risk of this type of cancer is significantly reduced by spay surgery before the onset of estrus.

Vaginal discharge (mucus, pus of any color) in cats of any age should receive veterinary attention as soon as possible. Vaginal discharge may be normal immediately following delivery of kittens, however, and may range in color from brownish-red to dark chocolate brown to greenish-brown—as long as the queen is behaving normally and the kittens are healthy this should not be of concern.

Bloody vaginal discharge is not normal during estrus or any other time in cats. During heat, the queen's vulva may be slightly swollen, she will be restless and vocal and she may be irritable and lose her appetite. *Do not allow her to roam anywhere outside your home until she is spayed (and even then she should remain a safe and happy house cat)!* Vaginal bleeding that is accompanied by discomfort, fever, loss of appetite, lethargy or agitation should prompt an emergency visit right away.

Vaginal discharge, discomfort, fever, loss of appetite, lethargy or restlessness in a queen after mating could be signs of infection. If your cat has these symptoms, call for an immediate appointment.

VAGINAL OR UTERINE PROLAPSE

The vagina and/or uterus may turn inside out and protrude to the outside of the body. Vaginal or uterine prolapse is an emergency situation that requires urgent veterinary intervention and surgery may be necessary. Left untreated, these conditions may become complicated by infection and obstructed blood supply. If your cat is distressed and licking at what looks like a red gelatinous cauliflower of any size (it may be quite large if the prolapse is uterine) protruding from the vulva, you should:

1. Flush with cold water gently poured over the pulpy mass. (Wear latex or rubber gloves if these are

available, otherwise you will need to use bare hands that are thoroughly washed.)

2. Sprinkle salt generously over the surface of the prolapse. After several minutes you should see the tissue begin to shrink; try to push the prolapse back into the vagina with several closed fingers (to avoid perforating the fragile tissues with just one finger).

3. If necessary, flush with cool water and salt and try to invert the prolapse once or twice more.

4. Regardless of whether you are successful, take your cat to a nearby veterinary facility right away. Cover the area with a clean damp towel to keep prolapsed tissues moist and to minimize contamination and trauma—even if you successfully reduced the prolapse, tissues can evert easily at any time so a damp towel will be a good thing to take along.

5. If the exposed tissue has any areas that are brown, black or green, or if you detect any tears or puncture wounds on the surface, be sure to inform the veterinary staff. In these cases, spay surgery may be unavoidable to save your cat.

SPAY YOUR FEMALE CAT

To prevent common emergencies in your female cat, have her spayed! You will dramatically decrease her risk of malignant mammary tumors (the equivalent of breast cancer in women) and eliminate complications of pregnancy and delivery, false pregnancy, uterine and vaginal infections, ovarian disease, unintended breeding and the addition of kittens to the tragic proportions of the pet overpopulation crisis.

After spay surgery, follow your veterinarian's advice carefully. If your cat normally roams free outside, keep her indoors until the sutures, if any, are removed or until your veterinarian agrees to return her activity to normal. Watch for any type of vaginal discharge or discharged from the incision site. If any sign of pain or discomfort is shown, call your veterinarian for further advice.

Complications following any surgery do occur, but serious complications are infrequent and should not discourage you from spaying your cat.

Mismating

Pregnancy may be undesirable in the queen for a number of reasons. She may be in poor physical health or too old to withstand giving birth. She may also be too young—a queen under 6 months or even 1 year of age is at a higher risk for complications at delivery. If a mismating has occurred and you would like to prevent fertilization, the following recommendations are offered:

1. See your veterinarian within forty-eight hours of mismating. Medication, by injection or by mouth, may be available to prevent pregnancy. It will also prolong the signs of "heat" and you will need to supervise her continually until all signs of heat disappear. This treatment will not prevent additional mismating!

2. As mentioned elsewhere in this book, get your cat spayed! Unless your cat is of particular breeding value, the preferred treatment of unintended mating is sterilization.

Poison Ingestion

Poisons can be found in common household items, such as bleach or houseplants, or in automotive supplies, such as antifreeze or motor oil. Pesticides and rodenticides are poisonous, as are many paints and shellac. Turpentine, kerosene, acetone (found in nail polish remover) and most cleaning fluids are dangerous to cats, as are medicines intended for human use (e.g. acetaminophen is lethal) and illicit drugs. Other potentially toxic items include children's crayons and shoe polish. Some food items, such as chocolate, can be lethal. Finally, some poisons are found in the environment and may be contaminants (such as lawn and garden herbicides or gasoline-polluted water) or naturally occurring (such as certain mushrooms or blue-green algae).

The specific treatment for poisoning will depend on the poison in question. Some poisons require specific treatments and antidotes, whereas others call for basic life support until the cat can clear the poison from her system. There are, however, general first aid steps that you can take immediately upon discovering that your cat has ingested a poisonous substance:

1. Induce vomiting by pouring ½ teaspoon of either hydrogen peroxide or table salt on the cat's tongue as close to the back of the throat as possible.

2. Collect a sample of your cat's vomit for laboratory analysis to identify an unknown poison.

POISONOUS ORNAMENTAL PLANTS

Amaryllis
Azalea
Black-eyed Susan
Bleeding heart
Cone flower
Chinaberry tree
Daffodil
Euonymus
Foxglove
Hemlock
Horse chestnut
Hyacinth
Hydrangea
Iris
Larkspur
Lily-of-the-valley
Mistletoe
Oleander
Poinsettia
Poppy
Rhododendron
Snow-on-the-mountain
Star-of-Bethlehem
Virginia creeper
Wisteria
Yew

Note: If your cat has swallowed a corrosive chemical, such as a solvent or cleaning fluid, *do not induce vomiting.*

> ## TAKE STEPS TO PREVENT POISONING
>
> Pet-proof your home as soon as you acquire a cat and maintain her safety for a lifetime! Search each room in your home and place toxic chemicals out of reach or locked away safely. Place safety latches on all cabinets that are accessible to your cat. Keep doors closed or use gates or screen doors to barricade your cat from areas of your home that might contain hazards. Minimize your use of poisonous substances altogether. Ask your mechanic to use pet-safe antifreeze. Remove dangerous plants from your home and your yard. Keep the telephone numbers of your regular veterinary clinic and local veterinary emergency center in plain view (on your refrigerator, for example) and on an index card in your cat's first aid kit. Include the hot line number of the National Animal Poison Control Center, (800) 548-2428 or (888)-4ANIHELP. This organization is available twenty-four hours a day, every day, all year, and is affiliated with the SPCA (Society for the Prevention of Cruelty to Animals). The charge for the call is about $30, but it will certainly be worthwhile in an emergency.

3. Call ahead and proceed calmly but without delay to the veterinary clinic.

If your cat has licked some of the substance adhered to her coat (look for heavy salivating and licking motion with her tongue) rinse her mouth liberally with repeated clear water flushes and call your veterinarian's office for further instructions.

If your pet seems to be behaving normally after contact with a suspected poison, call your veterinarian for further emergency instructions or contact the National Animal Poison Control Center at (800) 548-2428. Assuming that your veterinarian will want to see your cat, bring the prescription bottle of any ingested medication, the package label of the ingested poison or a sample of the suspected source of poisoning so that your veterinarian can administer the specific treatment whenever possible.

If your pet seems to be deteriorating despite your first aid, call your veterinary clinic to advise them that you will be arriving shortly and transport your pet *immediately* (along with anything that might identify the specific poison involved).

Heart Failure

Cardiac problems are relatively common in cats and obesity plays a significant role in the development and progression of heart disease. With regular exercise and a controlled diet, cats can maintain a healthy body weight for a lifetime. Congenital cardiac problems are common in cats but often respond well to treatment. Other diseases impact the healthy heart, however, such as heartworm disease and dental disease.

Regular vaccines and checkups are intended to promote your cat's health and prevent many potential problems. If your veterinarian discovers an irregular heartbeat or murmur, periodic visits, an electrocardiogram and a cardiac ultrasound may be advised. Cardiac medications and surgery are available to treat your cat just as in human medicine.

Keeping your cat active—even by enticing her to play with a roll of paper towels—will help her maintain a healthy body weight for a lifetime.

Heart failure can occur in cats with previously diagnosed heart problems but it can also happen to cats who were not considered at risk. Signs of possible heart failure can be confused with other diseases, such as respiratory infection, but may be suspected if the following are present:

- shortness of breath—rapid and shallow respiration

- coughing—particularly in the evening and overnight

- pale pink or bluish tongue—associated with shock or oxygen depletion

- exercise intolerance—decrease in stamina, coughing, wheezing, easy exhaustion, bluish tongue, fainting, loss of consciousness

- unusual heartbeat—rapid and weak, rapid and pounding or unusually slow

If your cat has developed any of the signs described above, call your veterinarian to be seen within twenty-four hours. If your cat is extremely lethargic, unable to rise and generally weak, see a veterinarian *immediately*. It is of vital importance to keep a cat in heart failure as calm as possible. Speak softly, drive carefully, and do not panic. If your cat is unconscious, with or without a history of heart disease, check for heartbeat and breathing:

1. If heartbeat and/or respiration are absent, administer cardiac massage and/or artificial respiration as necessary. Get help if possible and continue CPR en route to the clinic *immediately*.

2. If heartbeat and respiration are present, continue to monitor during transport. Cover your cat with a blanket and transport *immediately*.

chapter 5

Exposure
and Other
Environmental
Injuries

Your cat is exposed to many hazards when outside. Temperature extremes, for example, can be more than uncomfortable for your cat. He can suffer from serious heatstroke and hypothermia if left out in bad weather. These and many other dangers can be avoided by simply keeping your cat indoors. House cats lead happy and healthy lives. Responsible pet ownership will save you and your pet much unnecessary pain.

Contact with Aggressive Wildlife

Contact with wildlife can harm your cat in a number of ways.

RABIES

One of the most serious effects of being bitten by a wild animal is the possibility of contracting rabies. Rabies is a fatal disease caused by a virus that is transmitted by direct contact with the secretions (primarily saliva and blood) of infected animals. Rabid animals do not necessarily fit the image of the frenzied and agitated beast that froths at the mouth; the infected carrier may be only subtly affected at the time it comes in contact with your cat. This disease is highly contagious to all mammals, including people. Speak with your veterinarian and find out what your cat requires in the way of rabies vaccines and the interval between vaccinations. Keep these vaccines updated according to the recommendations in your area. Note that rabies is currently reported everywhere in the United States but there are regions where it has reached epidemic proportions. Some of the wildlife that may harbor this virus include the raccoon, fox, skunk and bat, but all mammals are vulnerable to rabies, from chipmunks to moose.

Rabies is a fatal disease. Keep your cat's vaccines up to date.

ATTACK

Even if your cat survives the attack and the animal is not rabid, bite wounds and scratches must be treated as if the offending wildlife was infected with the deadly rabies virus. The risk is too great to do otherwise.

These wounds have a high rate of bacterial infection and could require prolonged and painful treatment.

If your cat is attacked by a wild animal, use gloves and act quickly to disinfect any visible wounds with warm water and plenty of soap. Regardless of whether you detect an open wound, your veterinarian should be contacted regarding possible quarantine and a rabies vaccine booster. Please refer to other relevant topics elsewhere in this book, such as "Lacerations and Puncture Wounds" (chapter 3), "Disinfecting Wounds" and "Applying Bandages" (chapter 2).

Even though most cats can swim, they are susceptible to drowning.

Drowning

Although most cats will instinctively swim (and a few even enjoy it!), cats can and do drown. Cats may fall through thin ice into a frozen pond or be swept away in the current of a flooded river. A cat can drown in just a few inches of water because he need only aspirate enough water to obstruct the passage of air to the lungs. A sedated cat is particularly at risk for drowning, and a cat that is immersed to control heatstroke may survive his hyperthermia but not its treatment without careful handling in the water used to cool down his body temperature.

Fall Through Ice

If your cat has fallen into a frozen pond or lake, call for local authorities to help with your rescue. Tie yourself to a nearby tree or have someone hold you and stretch your body flat against the ice. Reach for your cat with a gloved hand (he may bite or scratch out of panic or fear) or use a rope that you can loop around his neck to pull him from the water. Regardless of how your cat

may have risked drowning (e.g. fallen overboard during a boat trip), make certain that your own safety is secured before jeopardizing your own life in order to save your cat. When reaching to pull your cat from the water, circumstances may prevent you from grasping the back of his neck. Grab onto any part of the cat that you can and do not let go; you may not have another chance.

BACK ON LAND

If your rescued cat is conscious, towel him dry and keep him warm; watch for any difficulty breathing

To expel water and debris from the cat's airway, hold him upside down by the hips and swing him in a wide arc.

(coughing, wheezing) or any decrease in appetite or level of activity. Near-drowning complications include polluted water and debris in the lungs and contact with bacterial or toxic contaminants. Any problem in the several days after a near-drowning experience should be reported to your veterinarian. To be safe, your cat should be examined the same day.

If your cat is unconscious when he emerges from the water:

1. Check his heartbeat and respiration; if both are present, towel dry, cover him with a dry blanket and transport him to the nearest veterinary facility *immediately.*

2. If heartbeat is present but the cat is not breathing, hold him upside down firmly by the hips and swing in a wide arc from side to side. Repeat several times to expel water and debris that may have entered the airways; lay the cat back down on his side and pull his tongue forward to check his

mouth for any material in the back of his throat. If the cat is too heavy or awkward for you to lift, lay him on his side with hips elevated and his head slanting downward; place one hand on the cat's chest with open palm and depress firmly downward and quickly release. Repeat several times as described above, removing any fluid or debris that may have collected in the cat's throat.

Check again for both heartbeat and respiration; proceed with artificial respiration with or without cardiac massage (see chapter 2).

3. If heartbeat and breathing are absent, begin CPR. If the chest does not rise and fall with each assisted respiration, repeat your attempts to clear the airways as described above—continue CPR and transport to the veterinary hospital *immediately*.

Cats are less likely to chew on electrical cords if they have entertaining diversions.

Electric Shock

Electrocution can occur inside as well as outside your home. Live wires can fall within reach of your pet and, although they are small targets, lightning can strike cats, too! Mischievous young cats commonly chew on wires and cables as they explore their environment.

Injuries from contact with electricity include burns (blackened skin, raw sores) at the lips, tongue, gums; burns at the point of contact (feet, back, nose, almost anywhere); infection; cardiac arrhythmia/arrest; respiratory arrest; and fluid in the lungs.

If your cat has received an electric shock, it is essential to give priority to life-threatening injuries. Do not worry about a burn, no matter how severe, if your cat's heart has stopped. You must act cautiously but quickly.

1. Evaluate the situation: Is your cat still in contact with live electric current? *Do not touch your cat until he is removed from the source of electricity!* If your cat is unconscious or awake but unable to move, use a nonmetal object (such as a broom handle or a toilet plunger) to push your cat away from the source. If your cat is conscious and able to walk, call him to come to you and away from the source of electricity. Turn off power to the offending electric source before entering the area to rescue or treat your injured cat and call the power company or fire department for help.

2. Check for heartbeat and respiration and administer CPR as necessary. Call for immediate assistance and transport your cat to the animal hospital *immediately.*

3. If your cat seems uninjured but is unusually quiet, call the clinic to let them know you are on the way; dangerous cardiac arrhythmias (irregular heartbeat) may be undetectable to you and must be corrected immediately.

4. If your cat seems to be active and alert but has sustained minor burns to his body surface, refer to chapter 3 for the discussion of treating burns. Carefully monitor your cat over the next several hours and maintain watchfulness for several days in case complications should develop. Any change in your cat's behavior or appearance warrants a call to your veterinary clinic for further instructions. It is

AVOID ELECTRICAL INJURIES BY PET-PROOFING

With young cats in particular, an important part of pet-proofing your home is to eliminate the risk of electrocution. Look around each room and think of ways to decrease the desire and opportunity to reach electric cords or wires:

- Cable covers may be purchased at hardware stores, computer stores or through specialty catalogs.

- Rearrange furniture to create obstacles to wiring, electric plugs and wall sockets.

- Place baby guards in unused wall sockets.

- If necessary, prevent access to rooms that seem hazardous; some cats will not jump baby gates but for those that do, keep the door closed or add a screened door to the room.

- Place upside-down mousetraps near attractive wires that will snap shut to startle the curious cat and create a negative association with the electric cords.

- Make sure your cat has enough daily exercise and playtime to become tired and content.

probably wise to call the animal hospital to report the incident even in the absence of any apparent injury and ask for further instructions.

Ingestion of Foreign Object

Young cats are notoriously curious. Part of their investigation of the world around them includes tasting, gnawing and playing with objects in their mouths—sometimes swallowing inappropriate objects. Some mature cats will do the same.

Kittens are known for their curiosity—keep hazardous objects out of their reach.

If you witness the ingestion of an inedible object, there are three options:

1. Do nothing: An object smaller than ½ inch in diameter and with a smooth surface may pass through uneventfully. There are, however, unsafe items that fit this description. Coins, particularly pennies, can corrode in the acid environment of the digestive system and release toxic metals. Tablets or pills prescribed for your own use could be toxic to your cat; induce vomiting (see below) and call your animal hospital for further instructions or call the National Animal Poison Control Center at (800) 548-2428.

2. Induce vomiting within fifteen minutes by sprinkling a teaspoon of salt or hydrogen peroxide on the back of the cat's tongue. Do *not* induce

vomiting of pointed or jagged items (such as a needle and thread) that could cause serious injury on the way back up.

3. Call the animal hospital and tell them you are on the way with your naughty kitten. Depending on what the object is, how long ago it was swallowed and what the radiograph or ultrasound shows, your veterinarian may induce vomiting, use special equipment to extract the object under anesthesia or perform emergency exploratory surgery.

Repeated vomiting may be caused by swallowing a foreign object but may also be caused by a variety of other maladies (see the discussion on vomiting in chapter 4).

PUT SMALL ITEMS OUT OF YOUR CAT'S REACH

The importance of pet-proofing cannot be over stressed.

To prevent your cat from swallowing inappropriate objects, place them out of the reach or store them away until the cat is more trustworthy and mature. Be particularly vigilant about small items such as decorative items, Christmas ornaments, children's toys and sewing kits. Remove objects that are attractive to chew such as pens, pencils, house plants, elastic bands and ribbons, among many more. Empty trash baskets daily or, better yet, keep them inaccessible by whatever means are necessary to protect your cat.

Hit by Car

If your cat has been hit by a car, give priority to the injury that would be fatal if left unattended. For example, a scraped elbow or broken tooth is less important than a fractured pelvis, which is less urgent than cardiac arrest; arterial bleeding from a lacerated ear is less crucial than hemorrhage from a major vein in the leg. *Always eliminate the possibility of an injury that is truly life-threatening by first evaluating the vital signs:*

1. Check for pulse and respiration; administer CPR as necessary.

2. Control bleeding with direct manual pressure until other materials become available (ice, tourniquet, veterinary care).

3. Keep the cat covered with a blanket or towel unless he is agitated. If the cat is conscious, reassure him with a calm voice and soothing tone. Stay in control so as not to further alarm your pet, and delay

any emotional reaction until your cat is delivered to the clinic for evaluation and treatment.

Note: Details on administering CPR, controlling bleeding and treating a cat for shock are set forth in chapter 2.

4. Even if your cat seems fine, proceed directly to the veterinary hospital; remember, many injuries may be silent and could be delayed.

Heatstroke

Heatstroke is an abnormally high body temperature (over 104°F) caused by prolonged exposure to a hot environment. A cat that is confined in a car in direct sunlight or left outside on a hot summer day without access to shade or water is at risk of heatstroke. In any situation where there is inadequate ventilation and overheating, heatstroke may result in a real life or death emergency.

Too much sun on a hot day can lead to heatstroke.

Signs of heatstroke include a body temperature higher than 104°F; fatigue, disorientation, lethargy and collapse (which may progress to seizure); vomiting and diarrhea; hyperventilating and heavy panting; very red gums (blood vessels will be very dilated at the surface to help give off more body heat). If your cat is showing most of these symptoms and has been in a situation that put him at high risk for heatstroke, you must act quickly to reduce body temperature:

Addressing
Emergencies

1. Measure his rectal temperature and verify it every fifteen to twenty minutes during treatment to monitor his progress.

2. Place him in the sink or bathtub in enough cool (not cold) water to cover his body. Support his head above the water in your hands (in advanced stages of collapse, the cat may be too weak or unconscious and could drown).

3. Place ice packs at the pads of the feet; rubbing alcohol on the feet will also cool the cat down quickly.

4. Drape an ice pack or bag of frozen vegetables on the cat's head for a few minutes at a time until his rectal temperature reads normal.

TO PREVENT HEATSTROKE

Very young kittens, geriatric cats and adult cats with a medical problem are not tolerant of hot weather. Keep your cat indoors when the mercury climbs too high. Better yet, keep your cat indoors indefinitely to avoid a long list of hazards and potential for harm to your cherished pet. If you must travel with your cat, offer him a drink frequently. Bring a container of water along with a face cloth and wet your cat's face, head and feet to cool him down. Wipe down his entire body with the damp cloth if he has a short coat before resuming travel—but be sure not to chill him with the air conditioner if you do.

Note: If the cat is not vomiting and is alert, you may offer water but not until he is alert and able to respond. When the cat is ready to drink, give him 1 or 2 teaspoons of water at a time at intervals of every fifteen minutes to be sure that he does not drink excessively and vomit.

If your cat's temperature drops to within normal range (below 103°F) and he seems to have fully recovered, call the animal hospital to report the incident and ask for further instructions.

Prevent heatstroke by keeping your cat inside during hot weather.

A professional evaluation may be called for, depending on the circumstances that created the heatstroke and the general health of your cat.

Despite your intervention, if your cat's temperature fails to decline at all within the first twenty minutes, if he has lost consciousness and does not respond in this time frame or if convulsions and tremors occur, take him to the nearest clinic *immediately*.

Hypothermia

Hypothermia is an abnormally low body temperature. A body temperature lower than 99°F is hypothermic, and the cat should receive emergency care. If the core temperature falls below 95°F, the cat is unlikely to recover. Prolonged exposure to cold and freezing temperatures, shock and excessively long periods immersed in water cooler than normal body temperature can cause hypothermia.

Shivering and trembling is the body's way of generating additional heat. In severe hypothermia, the cat may no longer be able to defend against drastic reduction in body heat, particularly if he is in the deep stages of shock. If your cat has been lost, missing or exposed to cold weather and seems extremely fatigued, cold to the touch, has pale gums or any sign of shock (see chapter 2) you should:

> ### HOW TO PREVENT HYPOTHERMIA
>
> Don't allow your cat to roam freely outdoors when temperatures fall. Temperatures under 50°F may be very hard on a cat, even if he has a long and thick coat, especially if he is very young or getting on in years. Do not leave your cat outdoors for longer than thirty minutes, even in your back yard, when temperatures dip below freezing. Cats can suffer from frostbite, too, and can fall through the thin ice of frozen ponds, rivers and lakes. On very cold days, most cats would prefer to stay indoors with you and your family where they belong and deserve to be. If your cat prefers to remain indoors during winter months, consider turning him into a house cat and confining him indoors where he will always be safe, even when the weather warms up.

1. Cover him with a towel that has been warmed in the dryer, an electric blanket (medium heat) or a thick blanket. Gently rub his legs and body to stimulate circulation (unless other injuries make this impractical).

2. Measure his rectal temperature (described in chapter 2).

3. Surround his back and belly with several plastic containers filled with hot water or hot water bottles (avoid heating pads unless covered with a thick towel or unless used for brief periods, because incapacitated animals cannot move away if it is too hot and could be burned). If the cat does not

have any injury that precludes this, you may wrap him inside your own clothing to share your body heat.

4. Measure rectal temperature every fifteen to twenty minutes—the cat's body temperature should reach the low normal range (about 100°F) within the hour.

Never leave your cat outdoors for more than thirty minutes in winter weather.

Note: If your cat does not improve substantially within one hour, if he remains immobile and does not shiver or if there are any other injuries apparent or suspected, see a veterinarian *immediately*.

Head
and Brain
Problems

Clearly, injuries to your cat's
head and other neurological
events require a quick response.
Do not hesitate to take your cat
to an emergency clinic under
these circumstances.

Ear Emergencies

Trauma, foreign objects and
infection are the most likely
causes of urgent ear problems. Traumatic injuries include lacerations (cuts) or puncture wounds (which are discussed in detail in
chapter 3). Even with minor wounds, injured ears frequently bleed
quite a bit, partly because the cat tends to shake her head and disturb clot formation!

TRAUMA TO THE EAR

In addition to cuts, ear infections (including ear mites), insect bites
and skin parasites can lead to traumatic injury of the ear. By repeated

Make an ear bandage with panty hose. Slide it over your cat's face until it fits around her head, securing the injured ear and gauze dressing close to the head.

head shaking or scratching, blood vessels can be broken in the pinna, or ear flap, and cause a pocket of blood between the skin and the ear cartilage referred to as an aural hematoma. These tubular swellings on the ear flap, secondary to trauma or infection, are not dangerous to the cat but may require non-emergency surgical repair. The aural hematoma will heal without surgery, but the ear may be rippled and twisted in appearance (the equivalent to the "cauliflower ear" of professional prize-fighters). A veterinarian must still see the underlying infection or injury as soon as possible.

If your cat's ear has a bleeding injury:

1. If the wound is minor and bleeding is minimal, disinfect the wound and apply direct manual pressure. Apply topical antibiotic. If any signs of infection develop over the next few days, have your cat examined within twenty-four hours. If bleeding cannot be controlled, see your veterinarian the same day.

2. If the wound is large or bleeding is not easily controlled, apply an ice pack along with direct manual pressure. Next, apply several layers of gauze squares to the injured site and fold the ear flat against the top of the cat's head. Make a bandage with an old sock (cut off the toe seam) or a length of lady's pantyhose and slide it over your cat's muzzle and face until it fits around the cat's head, holding the injured ear in place. Pass two fingers under the sock/stocking bandage to make sure it is not too tight. You can remove the bandage if it seems to make your cat anxious. Call the clinic for an appointment the same day.

If your cat develops a swelling on her ear flap:

1. Apply an ice pack to the ear for at least fifteen minutes several times a day until a veterinarian can evaluate her. Call the veterinary clinic for the earliest possible appointment.

2. Examine the inside of the ear and look for any kind of discharge, redness, odor or discomfort when you touch the ear.

3. Look inside the ear canal for any small object or debris (leaves or soil for example) that may have fallen inside—flush with warm water as discussed below.

4. Examine the outside of the ear for the presence of insect bites along the ear margins, ticks adhered to the skin anywhere near the ear, head or neck and fleas or signs of fleas in the region of the head or neck. Follow treatment instructions with appropriate medication from the animal clinic.

If your cat's ear seems to be very itchy, give a single dose of diphenhydramine, an over-the-counter antihistamine (6.25 mg for kittens and cats weighing less than 5 pounds and 12.5 mg for the adult cat; this is $\frac{1}{4}$ to $\frac{1}{2}$ of a 25 mg tablet or the corresponding amount in liquid form), to provide immediate relief. This works particularly well for insect bites and may help temporarily for minor infections as well. *Seek veterinary attention if any ear problem persists for more than twenty-four hours.*

If your cat's ear seems irritated, look inside the ear canal for a small object or debris.

EAR INFECTIONS

If your cat suddenly begins to scratch her ear, shake her head or rub her ear against the ground, it is possible that a foreign object has fallen into the ear canal. Lift the ear and examine the ear canal, using a small flashlight from your first aid kit. Remove any small object that may have fallen inside. If you cannot see anything or cannot reach what you find, flush the ear canal with several tablespoons of warm water—if something floats closer to the surface, use a pair of tweezers to gently extract it (the eardrum is angled deep within the canal and you will not perforate it!). If you are unable to extract the foreign body, call the clinic to be seen the same day.

Ear infections can develop quickly or gradually but, either way, they can become an emergency if the cat is extremely uncomfortable. If your pet is continually shaking her head, scratching at her ears, crying, has a fever, stops eating, loses her balance, seems unsteady and/or is walking in circles, make sure that she is seen within twenty-four hours. If your cat seems to have a minor ear infection, with symptoms such as redness, swelling, discharge, odor or pain in her ear(s), call for the next available appointment (within forty-eight hours). Ear mite infestation is very common and the discharge produced by these microscopic insects is dry, brown and abundant. Ear mites are very uncomfortable, and although not contagious to people, are very contagious between cats. Any sign of persistent discomfort deserves veterinary attention as soon as possible.

Eye Emergencies

The cat's eye is a delicate and exquisite instrument and is the largest eye, in proportion to the head, of all mammals. Non-specific signs of ocular pain or discomfort include blinking, squinting, refusal to open the eye, increased tear production and unusual discharge. Any persistent eye problem, regardless of how minor it may seem to you, should receive veterinary attention within twenty-four hours.

The major causes of ocular emergencies are trauma, foreign bodies, autoimmune problems and infection. These may involve the eyeball, the eyelids, the conjunctiva (the inside lining of the eyelids), the cornea (the clear surface layer of the eyeball) and the retina (the back of the eye). Any of these structures may be lacerated (torn), ruptured, punctured and may also hemorrhage. The eye socket may be fractured. The "white" of the eye (sclera) can become bloodshot, hemorrhagic or bumpy. Bacterial infection can invade a traumatic injury or complicate a viral infection. Glaucoma, one of the leading causes of blindness in cats, can occur spontaneously but it can also follow ocular infection or traumatic injury.

In glaucoma, the pupil (the adjustable opening that focuses light onto the retina) can become fixed in extreme dilation and the eye becomes painful, bloodshot and bulges as the internal pressure of the eye rises to produce a true ocular emergency.

Any persistent eye problem should been seen by a veterinarian within twenty-four hours.

OCULAR DISCHARGE

A cat's eyes produce clear tears that normally stain a deep mahogany color when they dry. Abnormal eye discharge ranges in color from white (usually mucus) to shades of yellow or green.

1. If fever, sneezing, coughing, loss of appetite, lethargy, itching or pain accompany the discharge, the cat should be seen by a veterinarian within twenty-four hours.

2. An ocular discharge with little or no sign of discomfort may be treated by flushing the eye once every six to eight hours in a twenty-four hour period with two or three drops of saline solution or sterile water. If there is little or no improvement after this time, however, contact your veterinarian without delay.

> ### IF YOUR CAT OBJECTS TO AN EYE EXAM
>
> The normal defense of the cat's eye is the blink reflex, and defenses become exaggerated when the eye is damaged. Examination of a cat's injured eye can be challenging, and if your cat becomes aggressive, do not insist on examining her further. Instead, call your veterinarian and have your cat seen the same day.

3. If the surface of the eye appears inflamed (blood-shot) and the inflammation persists for more than twenty-four hours despite flushes with saline, call for an appointment within twenty-four hours. If the inflammation is accompanied by discomfort of any kind, have the cat seen sooner.

FOREIGN BODY

If your cat suddenly seems to be blinking rapidly, squeezing her eye shut and the eye is tearing heavily, she may have a foreign body in her eye. Even small things, such as a speck of dust or an eyelash, can cause considerable inflammation.

1. Gently separate the eyelids and examine the eye-ball surface. Look inside the lining of the eyelids for any conspicuous material (you may see a fila-ment of thick mucus that has formed around a small foreign object to protect the eye).

2. Instill several drops of saline eye wash (from your first aid kit) to flush the eye; alternatively, a bottle of your own contact lens solution or clear cool water from the tap is appropriate. Use a cotton ball soaked in solution or water and squeeze it over the eye surface.

3. Separate the eyelids as best as you can. If you see the irritating material and it does not flush out, gently pry it out with a wet cotton ball. If your cat struggles and becomes increasingly agitated or irri-tated with you, leave her care to the professionals and have your cat seen right away.

4. If the eye seems less irritated after thorough flush-ing and the cat is comfortable, it is reasonable to wait an additional twenty-four hours before visiting the veterinarian; however, if minor discomfort per-sists, the cat should be seen as soon as possible. Clearly, if the discomfort is significant, either to you or to your cat, she should be taken to the clinic right away.

Note: Do not attempt to remove a foreign body that has penetrated the eye (not just floating on the surface).

Take your pet directly to the veterinarian. Do not risk causing additional damage or pain if foreign material is not easily extracted!

Cuts

If there is a laceration to the eyelid flush away debris with clear water (taking care not to flush debris into the eye itself). Apply ice directly to the cut eyelid even if there is little or no blood, to minimize swelling (the eye and associated structures swell easily, and the swelling alone increases discomfort and may prevent thorough examination). Call the clinic and tell them that you are on your way with a traumatic eye injury.

Cornea Problems

The cornea (the invisible, clear "skin" of the eyeball) may suffer from lacerations, punctures, foreign bodies, autoimmune diseases and infections. Suspected corneal problems should be evaluated within twenty-four hours. Symptoms to watch for include:

- blinking, squinting, refusal to open the eye
- increased tear production, unusual discharge
- white or gray spots, patches or streaks on the surface of the eyeball
- blood vessels that seem to creep over the surface of the eyeball or superficial changes in pigment (corneal invasion by pigment cells turns it brownish black—these inflammatory changes develop slowly over many days and weeks).

Eye Loss

Among the most shocking of emergencies is the eyeball that has been forced out of the eye socket (proptosis). This occurs most typically from blunt trauma. Proptosis can be partial or complete:

1. Do not try to replace the eyeball yourself!
2. Cover the eyeball and exposed eye socket with a sterile square gauze bandage that has been soaked in saline or water, preferably at room temperature.

3. Keep your cat calm and proceed directly to the nearest veterinary clinic.

Regardless of how ghastly a traumatic eye injury may appear, it is important to note that the same hazardous situation that injured the eye may have caused other injuries that are far more ominous. The eye is not a vital organ if the cat is in cardiac arrest or is bleeding heavily from a laceration in its leg. Always evaluate the possibility of an injury that is more life threatening as discussed elsewhere in this book. Priority must be given to the injury that would be fatal if left unattended.

> ## MAKE IT A HABIT TO EXAMINE YOUR CAT'S MOUTH
>
> Routine examination of your pet's mouth at least once each month is a good habit to acquire. You need not forcefully pry her jaws apart. Lift the lips or hold on to a favorite treat or toy while your cat nibbles at it. Look for firm and uniformly textured gums, clean teeth, normal pigment and breath. If there are any sudden or progressive changes, you will be able to recognize them. Watch for unusual positions of the tongue or jaw, constant licking movements, foul mouth odor, thick and constant drooling, bleeding, pawing or rubbing at the mouth or muzzle, gagging, coughing, pacing, restlessness and refusal to eat or drink. If your cat is showing any of these signs and becomes aggressive when you try to examine her mouth, do not insist any further— leave it to the professionals! Call your veterinarian for the earliest available appointment.

Oral Emergencies
BLEEDING FROM THE MOUTH

Bleeding from the mouth may be caused by trauma or a foreign body but can also be due to the loss of "baby teeth" (deciduous or "milk" teeth) in kittens or dental disease in adults. Kittens lose their "baby teeth" between 4 and 6 months of age, and, although they are usually swallowed with little bleeding, the canines and molars can sometimes bleed a bit. Bleeding due to tooth loss is no cause for alarm in kittens but should receive attention in cats over 6 months old who have their adult dentition. A fractured tooth is open to infection, and jagged edges may harm the cat's mouth. If your cat's teeth appear encrusted in plaque, stained, cracked, broken and bloody, or her gums seem to be unusually swollen, tender and bleed easily, schedule an appointment for a checkup as soon as possible. If these symptoms are accompanied by a fever or a decreased appetite, have your pet seen within twenty-four hours.

Gum Pigment Changes

The normal gum pigmentation in cats ranges from pink to pinkish-brown. Some cats have freckles on their lips but these generally do not extend into the mouth. Changes in pigment, from pink to black or pink to white, should be brought to your veterinarian's attention. Malignancy in the mouth may be more typically tumor-like but can also be a subtle change in pigment. Schedule a checkup at your earliest convenience.

Choking

Choking occurs with complete obstruction of the back of the throat (pharynx) or upper airways. This might happen if a small object, mouthful of food or a thick plug of mucus or saliva is inadvertently aspirated.

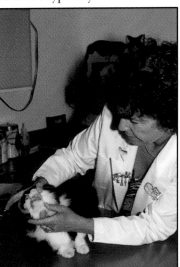

A choking animal cannot vocalize or make any sound at all because no air can pass from the lungs outward across the vocal cords to produce sound. A choking cat will make gagging movements with neck outstretched, open mouth, and have an increasingly blue tongue. Collapse and loss of consciousness will follow extreme distress within minutes. Respiratory arrest is the direct consequence of airway obstruction. Without immediate intervention, cardiac arrest follows.

Make it a habit to check your cat's teeth and mouth, including gum pigment changes.

Artificial respiration (and, therefore, CPR) will fail in a choking victim unless the obstruction is removed. It is critical to remove the obstruction to restore the airway. There are four basic techniques to dislodge obstructed foreign bodies in a cat's mouth or throat:

1. Check the inside of the mouth and throat. This step is reserved for the unconscious cat that is not breathing and when the chest does not inflate during artificial respiration. If the cat is still conscious,

proceed to the alternative techniques that follow. Do not stick your hands into a choking cat's mouth when she is in a state of panic. You risk unnecessary injury to yourself and will only exacerbate the cat's condition. As difficult as it may be, wait until the cat loses consciousness to explore her oral cavity:

- Pull the tongue forward and downward toward the cat's chest to dislodge any item that may be there.

- Reach with a bent index finger into the back of the cat's throat to feel for any object or material that might be obstructing the airway.

- If you see an object but cannot reach it, use a spoon or a pair of tweezers to do so, but be careful not to push it further into the airway.

- Be prepared to administer CPR immediately following removal of the obstruction.

2. The Heimlich maneuver is appropriate for conscious and unconscious choking cats:

- Lift the cat so that her back is against your chest.

- Make a fist with one hand so that the knuckle of the thumb rests against the cat's body and cover it with your other hand. Position your cupped hands in the middle of the belly just below the rib cage. With a sharp, upward thrust, squeeze your cupped hands into the cat's belly and release.

- For smaller cats, simply place one hand on either side of the belly just below the rib cage; squeeze and quickly release.

- Repeat if necessary; the obstructed object should be expelled with force.

- Check for heartbeat and breathing; administer CPR as needed and get veterinary help *immediately*.

3. An alternative method is to lay the conscious or unconscious cat on her side:

- Place the palm of one hand on the chest over the last few ribs.

- With a sharp, downward thrust, press into the cat's chest and release.

- If the cat is unconscious and the object is not visibly expelled from the mouth, open the mouth and sweep the back of the mouth and throat with a bent index finger in case the obstruction has dislodged but remains in the oral cavity.

- Check for heartbeat and breathing; administer CPR as needed and get veterinary help *immediately*.

4. A final method is simply to hold the cat upside down with her belly facing away from you. Encircle her hips with your arms and swing the cat back and forth—this is most effective when combined with the methods above, alternating as necessary to restore a patent airway.

Coughing

Coughing occurs when the respiratory system is irritated (such as from smoke or chemical fume inhalation), infected, infested (such as with parasitic worms) or inflamed (autoimmune or allergy-related responses). Coughing can also be due to a build-up of fluid in the lungs and airways, which occurs when the heart fails to function normally, for example, in heartworm disease or heart failure.

To perform the Heimlich maneuver, position your hands (hand over fist with thumb pressing inward) in the middle of the belly, just below the rib cage.

Coughing due to hairballs is not really coughing at all. Partial or total obstruction in the digestive tract by plugs of hair swallowed during grooming can lead to considerable local inflammation. This triggers a sort of gagging cough that represents the cat's efforts to dislodge the hairball. If that doesn't work, vomiting may bring the obstructed hair back up. It can sometimes be difficult to distinguish between a hairball "cough" and a cough originating in the respiratory system. Any cough that persists longer than two or three days should be brought to your veterinarian's attention.

If your cat's cough began within the last week or so, she may have an upper respiratory infection (a "common cold" to us). If sneezing and/or teary eyes accompany your cat's cough, she probably has an upper respiratory infection that could be contagious to other cats. Keep her confined to your home if she is an "outdoor" cat. Make sure that her vaccines are kept current every year through her lifetime.

If your cat is coughing but seems otherwise unaffected (alert, good appetite, active and playful as usual) wait a few days to see if the coughing improves; if coughing persists or worsens, call for a checkup without further delay.

If your cat is coughing and has a fever, decreased or no appetite, seems sluggish and withdrawn, anxious or uncomfortable, call for an appointment within twenty-four hours.

If your cat coughs mostly or exclusively in the evening or overnight, cardiac disease should be considered among the list of possible causes. Call for an appointment as soon as possible (sooner if your cat's health or attitude seems affected in any other way).

Convulsions

A convulsion, also referred to as a seizure or "fit," is a sudden and involuntary muscular contraction or series of muscular contractions. A convulsion may last for a few seconds or it may continue for many minutes. It may affect only a small body area (petit mal seizure or Jacksonian seizure). For example, the cat may appear to stumble or her jaw may chatter uncontrollably for a brief moment. She may appear to chase an invisible fly. If a seizure is caused by abnormal electrical activity in the emotional centers of the brain (such as during a psychomotor seizure) a sudden mood swing of aggressiveness may be triggered. Convulsions can also cause the cat to collapse and lose consciousness during massive and violent spasms. Occasionally, major generalized seizure activity will continue for prolonged periods (grand mal seizure) and require intensive veterinary care.

A seizure may happen just once or only a few times and never recur. Alternatively, seizure activity can occur sporadically over a lifetime or convulsions can progress and become more frequent, more intense and longer in time. If seizures are a symptom of a disease, it is important to try to pinpoint the cause of the seizure in case the illness can be treated. If seizures are due to epilepsy (abnormal zones of electrical activity in the brain) or to untreatable causes, anti-convulsant (anti-epileptic) drugs may be recommended for the remainder of your cat's lifetime.

If your cat is already on anti-convulsant medication and has a seizure that is worse than usual or has a cluster of seizures within a single day or several days, call your veterinarian for advice or have your cat seen right away (depending on the severity of the episodes). The goal of these medications is to reduce the number and severity of seizures. To cure seizure activity completely is the ideal outcome but is usually not realistic, especially in primary epilepsy.

If you think that your cat is having a seizure, do *not put your fingers or anything else in her mouth!* Your cat will not "swallow her tongue" during a convulsion, but you could be seriously injured by the involuntary movements of her jaw.

1. Move the cat only if she has collapsed in a precarious place, such as at the foot of the stairs, near a swimming pool or in the street.

2. Do not cover her with a blanket—body temperature rises during convulsions, and excess body heat should be allowed to escape.

3. Look at your watch and try to time how long the seizure lasted. This could be helpful information for your veterinarian.

4. After convulsing has stopped, verify heartbeat and respiration. If heartbeat and/or respiration are absent, administer CPR and seek veterinary attention *immediately*.

5. If the cat's heartbeat and respiration are stable, measure her body temperature. If her rectal temperature is elevated (up to 104°F is not uncommon immediately after a seizure), pour cool water over the pads of your cat's feet every few minutes and recheck rectal temperature after fifteen and thirty minutes to make sure that she has begun to cool down (stop when her temperature is under 103°F).

EMERGENCY CONVULSIONS

Your cat should be brought to see a veterinarian *right away* if:

- she has collapsed into generalized spasms that continue for longer than five minutes

- her tongue takes on a bluish hue during or after the seizure

- she has any difficulty breathing during or after the seizure

- she does not rise long after muscular contractions have disappeared (in the few moments after convulsions have ceased, your cat may remain dazed for about fifteen or twenty minutes and may seem tired for a few hours afterwards) or if lethargy persists more than three hours after the seizure

- rectal temperature has fallen but is still not within normal range (less than 103°F) one hour after the episode is over and your cat is still very lethargic

- she has a second seizure within twenty-four hours

- she has been previously diagnosed with any of the illnesses that cause convulsions listed above

Coma

Coma is complete loss of consciousness. The cat may appear to be asleep but *cannot be aroused.*

If you discover that your cat is unconscious and cannot be revived by calling her name or rubbing your knuckles on her ribcage:

1. Verify the presence of a heartbeat and respiration; administer CPR if needed.
2. Determine whether your cat has suffered a head or spinal injury. If this is suspected, transport with great care using a stretcher if possible.
3. Control any obvious bleeding injury.
4. Go to your veterinarian's office *immediately.*

Unlike these sleeping cats, comatose cats cannot be revived!

Fainting

Fainting (syncope) occurs when consciousness is suddenly and momentarily lost. Your cat may faint if the brain's oxygen supply drops, for example, when the heart rhythm is abnormal and blood is not pumped efficiently. Fainting itself is not a real emergency, however, the reason underlying the episode may become one. Did the cat simply stumble and fall, or did she have a brief seizure or some other neurological or cardiovascular problem? Perhaps the cat merely lost her balance because of an inner ear problem. If heart failure is responsible for the loss of consciousness, then

Addressing
Emergencies

the cat eventually could develop urgent symptoms associated with cardiac disease. Fainting also can become an emergency if the animal injures herself while falling, perhaps because she fell in an awkward position or tumbled down the stairs. Head injuries and lacerations, for example, may be consequences of fainting.

If your cat suddenly drops down to lie on her side or her belly, call her name to see if she responds to you. Are the eyes open or closed? If the eyes are open, does she blink when you pass your hands before her eyes? If the cat is simply dazed, reassure her with your voice to keep her calm and give her a few moments to recover. If the cat seems all right, schedule a checkup as soon as possible.

If the cat does not respond to you, rub her rib cage with your knuckles briskly to stimulate a response. If the cat regains consciousness but is unable to rise within five or ten minutes, have her examined by a veterinarian right away.

If the cat does not regain consciousness when you rub her rib cage, *immediately* check for heartbeat and respiration. Administer CPR if necessary, cover her with a blanket and transport her to the veterinarian's office *immediately.*

chapter 7

Bone Injuries

Bone injuries can be very serious and are always painful. If you think (or know) that your cat has suffered a broken bone, try to remain calm and remember to approach your cat with caution (see chapter 1 for tips on approaching an injured or ill cat).

Broken Bones

There are two major categories of broken bones, or fractures. An open fracture is one in which the bone fragments protrude at the skin surface.

A closed fracture remains hidden beneath the skin but should be suspected if an animal is unable or reluctant to bear weight on the injured limb. A fractured tail may hang limply or be pressed tightly between the legs. Closed fractures can be extremely damaging. A fractured rib, for example, could puncture a lung or lacerate the heart. A fractured skull can be fatal.

Closed fractures are further classified as "stable" or "unstable." In a stable fracture, the bone fragments

For some injuries, such as an open fracture, the best splint may simply be a folded towel placed under the limb during transport.

remain relatively interlocked and normally aligned. If the fracture involves a limb, the cat may even attempt to walk. This type of fracture must be distinguished from severe sprains, dislocations and other soft tissue inflammation that can be, at least initially, as disabling as a broken bone. In general, however, the pain of broken bones will deter voluntary movement of the limb. A stable fracture may not be visible on radiographs (x-rays) until several days after injury. A fracture is unstable when the bone fragments are out of normal alignment and function is impossible.

FIRST AID FOR AN OPEN FRACTURE

If your cat has an open fracture or wound:

1. Pour sterile water *only* (no antiseptic of any kind) over the surface to flush away dirt and debris. Avoid touching the wound with anything but the water and the dressing that will follow. Be careful not to dislodge bone fragments that might be viable for fracture repair, and do not touch the bone or wound with your hands.

2. Apply a non-stick sterile dressing, if possible, and cover with a light bandage.

3. If the wound is bleeding, disinfection is of secondary importance. An ice pack can be placed over the sterile dressing and loosely bandaged around the site. If bleeding is profuse, you may need to apply a tourniquet.

4. Place a folded towel beneath the limb during transport. A lightweight splint (such as cardboard or newspaper) may be helpful for added stability during transport as well as to prevent further damage and pain; however, a splint is not essential.

5. See a veterinarian *immediately*. (See chapter 2 on how to transport a pet that cannot walk.)

FIRST AID FOR A CLOSED FRACTURE

If there is a closed fracture:

1. Apply ice (optional) and a splint (limbs only); alternatively, loosely apply a very thick bandage (not tight, just thick—the layers will provide support and prevent swelling) to provide cushioning during immediate transport.

2. If your cat resents manipulation of the injury, *leave it alone*. Place a folded towel beneath the limb during transport.

DO NOT TRY TO RESET A BONE

Regardless of the type of break your cat incurs (open or closed), do not try to reset a broken bone yourself! You could cause additional damage and complicate the injury!

---

3. See your veterinarian right away. There may be nothing you can do other than to transport your cat to the nearest veterinary facility, especially if your cat has broken his jaw, skull or spine.

Limping

Limping, or lameness, implies an uneven gait. Laceration, infection, foreign body joint disease and tumors are some of the problems that may affect the feline leg from toenail to shoulder blade. In addition, neurological disorders and autoimmune disease may produce limping. Limping may appear gradually and remain unchanged or worsen progressively over many days and weeks. The latter condition would be typical of arthritis or a growth that impedes movement. Limping can also appear suddenly (due to a cat fight-related injury or a sprain, for example) and be associated with varying degrees of discomfort or pain.

*Moderate lameness
is associated with
frequent stops to
sit and rest, or to
take weight off of
the affected leg.*

Lameness is considered mild if the cat still bears weight on the affected leg most of the time but normal motion is impeded. Moderate lameness is associated with intermittent non weight-bearing positions such as frequent stops to sit and rest, or brief pauses to raise the leg off the ground. A limp is severe if the cat is unable or unwilling to bear weight on the leg. Be careful when you examine an injured leg in case you unintentionally harm your cat and he instinctively tries to defend himself. Some cats may be very stoic when in pain until you touch the spot that hurts! Keep your wits about you and remain as objective as you can when your cat is in trouble.

Although there are many reasons why a cat might become lame, the same basic approach applies to most cases. Evaluate the whole cat first before focusing on the leg. Is the cat alert, breathing well, behaving normally? Attend to the most serious condition first. If your cat's leg was injured because he was hit by a car, for instance, it is far more important to look for signs of shock or to address profuse bleeding, than to examine the injured leg. If your cat is fine except for lameness, you may proceed to examine his leg more closely.

FIRST AID FOR LAMENESS

Systematically check the affected leg from the bottom to the top of the limb.

1. Closely examine the cat's feet:
   - Hold the paw, without squeezing or twisting it, and gently separate the toes to examine between them; do the same under the foot and examine each foot pad. Look for any crack or cut on the foot pads or the skin between them.
   - Make sure there is no red, moist or swollen area or any unusual smell.

- Check for the presence of any penetrating splinter or foreign object, such as a sticky burr or insect stinger.

- Examine the toes one by one for broken, bleeding or infected toenails. (See the discussion in chapter 3 concerning paw injuries.)

2. If you find no obvious reason for lameness (and even if you do), wrap your fingers gently around the cat's leg. With slight pressure moving upward toward the shoulder, feel for any swelling, painful area or wound between the foot and the shoulder. Apply first aid as needed.

3. Sudden lameness associated with moderate or extreme discomfort, loss of appetite, laceration, puncture wound, swelling (with or without discharge), suspected fracture or fever should be seen by a veterinarian on an emergency basis.

- Apply first aid appropriate to the situation (e.g. ice pack for swelling, direct manual pressure for bleeding or a splint for a fractured limb).

4. If your cat is limping just a bit but seems otherwise unaffected (no visible wound; normal temperature, appetite and behavior), it seems reasonable to wait two or three days (but no longer) before a veterinary examination to see whether the problem resolves on its own. During that time, however, you should:

Carefully inspect the feet and feel along the length of the legs— compare both sides to detect any changes on the injured limb.

- Restrict your cat's exercise. If your cat remains confined indoors, try to keep him in one room and discourage very active play. If your cat goes outside, keep him indoors for at least three days (and consider keeping him indoors indefinitely to prevent more serious problems).

- If the lameness persists beyond just a few days, seems to be getting worse or is affecting your cat in any other way, call to schedule a veterinary appointment within twenty-four hours.

Lameness frequently signals pain in cats and should not be allowed to continue when timely diagnosis and appropriate treatment could relieve the discomfort. Any persistent, continual or intermittent change in gait, regardless of your cat's age, should be brought to your veterinarian's attention. Call your veterinary clinic to report your concern about any problem, no matter how minor it may seem, for additional recommendations.

Spinal Injuries

The spine is a column of many small bones called vertebrae that are loosely fitted together. It begins at the base of the skull and extends to the tip of the tail. The spine functions to encase the spinal cord. Between each vertebra are the intervertebral disks that act as cushions to buffer the vertebra during movement and to protect the delicate spinal cord.

Spinal problems that may result in emergency situations include infections, trauma and congenital diseases that may affect the vertebrae, spinal cord or intervertebral disks. These may result in intense pain or no pain, spastic motion or paralysis, chronic degeneration or even instant fatality.

Infections of the spinal cord and column are most commonly due to viruses and bacteria, although other infectious agents may be the cause. These infections may be diffuse over the length of the spine, such as in meningitis, or they may be local, such as abscesses. The cat may or may not develop a fever but he is almost always in considerable pain. Depending on the nervous pathways that are impacted, the cat's ability to move or to feel may be affected.

Traumatic injury to the spine can result in dislocation or fracture of the vertebra or disks. This in turn may cause hemorrhage and swelling of the spinal cord and nerve branches and result in temporary or permanent nerve damage. Trauma may also sever the spinal cord.

A severed spinal cord at the neck is often fatal. A severed spinal cord below the neck may result in paralysis. Traumatic injury to the tail is often painful but will have the least significant consequences. Traumatic spinal injuries in cats are most often related to being hit by motor vehicles but can also occur by falling from heights or can be secondary to attacks by other animals.

Take your cat to the veterinarian immediately if you suspect that he has sustained traumatic injury to the spine.

Cervical (neck) injuries may be indicated if your cat holds his neck rigidly and slightly downward and moves gingerly. His appetite may decrease. Your cat may refuse to jump onto or off the bed or sofa as usual, and may avoid walking up or down stairs or simply remain inactive and subdued.

Also look for whether your cat walks more stiffly than normal, has difficulty walking in a straight line, seems to stumble, wobble or swagger (especially at the hind legs), whether he is very slow to rise or to lay down again, whether he holds his tail down persistently or resents having his tail lifted. Finally, note whether your cat reacts in pain if his head, neck or back is touched.

If your cat shares any of these symptoms, do not delay calling your veterinary clinic for an appointment right away. Your veterinarian will need to exclude the possibility of many other conditions with the same or similar signs. If your cat has been in any type of traumatic situation, bring him to a veterinary facility immediately.

119

First Aid for a Cat Unable to Rise

If your cat is unable to rise and remains lying down:

1. Make sure he can respond to you (is conscious). Evaluate the unconscious cat for the presence of heartbeat and respiration, administer CPR if necessary. If there is a hemorrhaging wound apply a pressure bandage and dressing, as necessary.

2. Cover him with a towel or light blanket if he is unconscious or shows any signs of shock.

3. Lift your cat slowly and carefully. It is usually best to carry him laying on his side (rather than cradled like a baby), with his legs upward, especially if spinal injury is suspected. Keep the spinal column as immobile as possible by passing your hand under the head and his body supported by the length of your arm.

4. If possible, slide a stretcher or blanket under your cat for *immediate* transfer to the clinic. If you do not have a stretcher, do not remove your cat from your vehicle when you arrive at the clinic—notify the staff of your arrival and they will take care of the rest.

Beyond the Basics

8

Resources

Allport, Richard. *Heal Your Cat the Natural Way.* New York: Howell Book House, 1997.

Carlson, Delbert G. and James M. Giffin. *The Cat Owner's Home Veterinary Handbook.* New York: Howell Book House, 1995.

Church, Christine. *Housecat: How to Keep Your Indoor Cat Sane and Sound.* New York: Howell Book House, 1998.

Commings, Karen. *Shelter Cats.* New York: Howell Book House, 1998.

DeBitetto, James, DVM. *Practical Kitten Care: An Easy-to-Use Guide for the Health and Care of Your Kitten.* New York: Howell Book House, 1996.

Edney, Andrew. *ASPCA Complete Cat Care Manual.* New York: DK Publishing, 1992.

Evans, Mark, MRCVS. *Cat Doctor.* New York, Howell Book House, 1996.

———. *Kitten Care.* New York: Howell Book House, 1996.

Evans, J.M. and Kay White. *The Catlopedia: A Complete Guide to Cat Care.* New York: Howell Book House, 1997.

Fogel, Bruce, DVM. *The Cat's Mind: Understanding Your Cat's Behavior.* New York: Howell Book House, 1992.

Foster, Race, DVM and Marty Smith, DVM. *The Complete Cat Health Manual.* New York: Howell Book House, 1997.

Gebhart, Richard H. *The Complete Cat Book: Expert Advice on Every Phase of Cat Ownership.* New York, Howell Book House, 1991.

Hawcroft, Tim, B.V.Sc. (Hons), M.A.C.V.Sc. *First Aid for Cats: The Essential Quick-Reference Guide.* New York: Howell Book House, 1994.

Humphries, Jim, D.V.M. *Dr. Jim's Animal Clinic for Cats: What People Want to Know.* New York: Howell Book House, 1994.

McGinnis, Terri. *The Well Cat Book.* New York: Random House, 1993.

Schwartz, Stefanie. *Instructions for Veterinary Clients: Canine and Feline Behavior Problems* (2nd ed.). New York: Mosby-Year Book, Inc., 1997.

————. *No More Myths: Real Facts to Answer Common Misbeliefs about Pet Problems.* New York: Howell Book House, 1996.

Siegal, Mordecai (ed). *The Cornell Book of Cats* (2nd ed.). New York: Villard Books, 1997.

Thornton, Kim Campbell and John Hamil, DVM. *Your Aging Cat: How to Keep Your Cat Physically and Mentally Healthy into Old Age.* New York: Howell Book House, 1996.

Viner, Bradley, MRCVS. *A-Z of Cat Diseases & Health Problems.* New York: Howell Book House, 1998.

Magazines

Animal Watch
(published by the ASPCA)
424 East 92nd St.
New York, NY 10128
(212) 876-7700

Cat Fanciers' Newsletter
304 Hastings
Redlands, CA 92373

Cat Fancy
P.O. Box 6050
Mission Viejo, CA 92690
(714) 855-8822

Catnip
Newsletter of Tufts University Medical Center
P.O. Box 420014
Palm Coast, FL 32142-0014
(800) 829-0926

Cat World International
P.O. Box 35635
Phoenix, AZ 85069
(602) 995-1822

Humane and Advocacy Groups

Alley Cat Allies
P.O. Box 397
Mount Ranier, MD 20712
(provides assistance for stray cats)

American Humane Association
Animal Protection Division
63 Iverness Dr. East
Englewood, CO 80112
(303) 792-9900

American Society for the Prevention of Cruelty to
Animals (ASPCA)
424 East 92nd St.
New York, NY 10128
(212) 246-2096

Delta Society
321 Burnett Ave. South, 3rd floor
Renton, WA 98055-2569
(206) 226-7357
(promotes the human-animal bond)

Friends of Cats
15587 Old Highway 80
El Cahor, CA 92021
(619) 561-0361

The Fund for Animals
200 W. 57th St.
New York, NY 10021
(212) 246-2096

Humane Society of the United States
2100 L St. NW
Washington, DC 20037
(202) 452-1100

I Love Cats
950 Third Ave., 16th Floor
New York, NY 10022-2705
(212) 628-7100

Morris Animal Foundation
45 Inverness Dr.
East Englewood, CO 80112-5480
(800) 243-2345

Pets for Patient Progress
P.O. Box 143
Crystal Lake, IL 60039-9143
(815) 455-0990

Pets for People
Call the animal shelter in your area or call (314) 982-3028 for information.

POWARS (Pet Owners with AIDS/ARC Resource Service, Inc.)
1674 Broadway
Suite 7A
New York, NY 10019
(212) 246-6307

Tree House Animal Foundation, Inc.
1212 W. Carmen Ave.
Chicago, IL 60640-2999
(312) 784-5488

Online Resources

American Animal Hospital Association
http://www.healthypet.com

American Association of Cat Enthusiasts
http://www.aaceinc.org

American Cat Fancier's Association
http://www.acfacat.com

American Veterinary Medical Association
http://www.avma.org/care4pets/

http://www.avma.org/netvet
An outstanding reference for everything about pets and many aspects of their care!

http://www.avma.org/resources
Easy access to hot topics such as poisons, rabies and much much more!

Canadian Cat Association
http://www.cca-afc.com

Cat Fancier's Association
http://www.cfainc.org

Dr. Stefanie Schwartz's Web site
http://www.dr-cookie.com,
Offers tips, advice and consultations in pet behavior problems.

Index

Abscesses, 46–49
Accidents, 14, 20, 92–93
Allergic reactions, 58–61
Anal glands, infected, 47
Approaching a frightened or injured cat, 8–12
Artificial respiration, 39–43, 47, 89
Aural hematoma, 98

Bandages, 26–27
Bites, 53
  insect, 58–61
  wild animal, 85–87
Bladder infections, 77–78
Bleeding (hemorrhage), 23–24, 26–27, 28, 54, 63, 114. *See also* Lacerations
  from the mouth, 104
  vaginal, 79
Blood pressure, 17, 20
Bone injuries, 113–20
Breathing (respiration), 15–17
Burns and scalds, 55–57

Cardiac disease, 108
Cardiac massage, 39, 42–43, 89
Cardiac problems, 82–84
Cardiopulmonary resuscitation (CPR), 84, 92, 105, 106, 107, 110, 112
  how to give, 39–43
Carrying an injured cat, 30–32
Cars
  confinement in, 93
  injuries from, 6, 92–93, 116, 119
Cervical (neck) injuries, 119
Choking, 105–7
Collar, Elizabethan, 62–63
Coma, 111
Consciousness, loss of, 14, 19, 75, 83, 94, 105–7, 109, 111–12
Constipation, 72–73
Convulsions, 75, 93, 95, 108–10
Cornea problems, 103
Coughing, 83, 88, 107–8

CPR (cardiopulmonary resuscitation), 84, 92, 104–7, 110, 112
  how to give, 39–43
Cuts. *See* Lacerations

Defecating, difficulty, 14
Dental disease, 83, 104
Diabetes, 74–76
Diarrhea, 70–72
Diphenhydramine, 99
Disinfecting wounds, 22–25, 89
Drowning, 87–89
Drug sensitivities, 76

Ear problems, 97–100
Ear medication, giving, 37–38
Electrical injuries, 89–91
Elizabethan collar, 62–63
Emergencies
  identifying, 13
  practicing for, 7–8
Epilepsy, 109
Eye emergencies, 14, 100–104
Eye medication, giving, 36–37

Fainting, 83, 111–12
False pregnancy, 80
Fever, 47, 50, 53, 56, 64, 67, 70, 75, 78, 79, 100, 101, 104, 108, 117
First aid, definition and goals of, 5–7
First aid kit, 7
Fleas, 59, 61
Foreign objects
  in eyes, 102–3
  ingestion of, 91–92
  in mouth or throat, 40, 105–7
  in paws, 64
  in wounds, 22
Fractures, 113–15
  splints for, 28–30, 114, 115

Glaucoma, 101
Glucose, 74–75
Gums, color of, 18, 20, 93, 95, 105